Best Ev

Science and the Bibl

BEST PROOF OF CREATION • DOES ASTRONOMY CONFIRM A YOUNG UNIVERSE?

SCIENCE OR THE BIBLE? • HOW OLD DOES THE EARTH LOOK?

10 BEST EVIDENCES FROM SCIENCE THAT CONFIRM A YOUNG EARTH

A POCKET GUIDE TO . . .

Best Evidences

Science and the Bible refute millions of years

Petersburg, Kentucky, USA

Reprinted January 2016

ISBN: 978-1-60092-763-8

Printed in China.

AnswersInGenesis.org

Table of Contents

Introduction

In many ways the age of the earth is an even more foundational issue for Christians than that of evolution. For if the earth is only thousands of years old, as the Bible indicates, then there's not nearly enough time for evolution to have happened. As a famous Harvard biologist once wrote:

> Time is in fact the hero of the plot. The time with which we have to deal is of the order of two billion years. What we regard as impossible on the basis of human experience is meaningless here. Given so much time, the "impossible" becomes possible, the possible probable, and the probable virtually certain. One has only to wait: time itself performs the miracles.

Take away the billions of years, and evolutions crumbles.

Recent findings in geology, astronomy, and other sciences consistently point to an earth that is much younger than the 4.5 billions years touted by secularists today.

This *Pocket Guide to Best Evidences* will aid you in understanding the foundational nature of the issue, will explore various dating methods that confirm a young earth, and will show you that when you start from biblical presuppositions, and look at the "evidence" through the lens of Scripture, you can come to solid conclusions that are not only true to the scriptural record, but also agree with sound science.

The Best Proof of Creation

by Ken Ham

In the ongoing war between creation and evolution, Christians are always looking for the strongest evidence for creation. They are looking for the "magic bullet" that will prove to their evolutionist friends that creation is true and evolution is false. This craving for evidence has led some Christians to be drawn to what we might call "flaky evidence." Over the past several years, some so-called evidence for creation has been shown not to be reliable. Some of these are

- supposed human and dinosaur footprints found together at the Paluxy River in Texas;

- the small accumulation of moon dust found by the Apollo astronauts;

- a boat-like structure in the Ararat region as evidence of Noah's Ark;

- a supposed human handprint found in "dinosaur-age rock";

- a dead "plesiosaur" caught near New Zealand.

Most well-meaning, informed creationists would agree in principle that things which are not carefully documented and researched should not be used. But in practice, many of them are very quick to accept the sorts of facts mentioned here, without asking too many questions. They are less cautious than they might otherwise be, because they are so keen to have "our" facts/ evidences to counter "theirs." What they really don't understand, however, is that it's not a matter of "their facts vs. ours." All facts are actually interpreted, and all scientists actually have the same observations—the same data—available to them.

Evidence

Creationists and evolutionists, Christians and non-Christians, all have the same facts. Think about it: we all have the same earth, the same fossil layers, the same animals and plants, the same stars—the facts are all the same.

The difference is in the way we all interpret the facts. And why do we interpret facts differently? Because we start with different presuppositions; these are things that are assumed to be true without being able to prove them. These then become the basis for other conclusions. All reasoning is based on presuppositions (also called axioms). This becomes especially relevant when dealing with past events.

Past and present

We all exist in the present, and the facts all exist in the present. When one is trying to understand how the evidence came about—Where did the animals come from? How did the fossil layers form? etc.—what we are actually trying to do is to connect the past to the present. However, if we weren't there in the past to observe events, how can we know what happened so that we can explain the present? It would be great to have a time machine so that we could know for sure about past events.

Christians, of course, claim they do have, in a sense, a time machine. They have a book called the Bible, which claims to be the Word of God who has always been there and has revealed to us the major events of the past about which we need to know. On the basis of these events (creation, the Fall, the Flood, Babel, etc.), we have a set of presuppositions to build a way of thinking which enables us to interpret the facts of the present.

Evolutionists have certain beliefs about the past/present that they presuppose (e.g., no God, or at least none who performed acts of special creation), so they build a different way of thinking to interpret the facts of the present.

Thus, when Christians and non-Christians argue about the facts, in reality they are arguing about their interpretations based on their presuppositions.

That's why the argument often turns into something like:

"Can't you see what I'm talking about?"

"No, I can't. Don't you see how wrong you are?"

"No, I'm not wrong. It's obvious that I'm right."

"No, it's not obvious."

And so on.

These two people are arguing about the same facts, but they are looking at the facts through different glasses.

It's not until these two people recognize the argument is really about the presuppositions they have to start with that they will begin to deal with the foundational reasons for their different beliefs. A person will not interpret the facts differently until he or she puts on a different set of glasses—which means to change one's presuppositions.

A Christian who understands these things can actually put on the evolutionist's glasses (without accepting the presuppositions as true) and understand how he or she looks at facts. However, for a number of reasons, including spiritual ones, a non-Christian usually can't put on the Christian's glasses—unless he or she recognizes the presuppositional nature of the battle and is thus beginning to question his or her own presuppositions.

It is, of course, sometimes possible that just by presenting "evidence" one can convince a person that a particular scientific argument for creation makes sense on "the facts." But usually, if that person then hears a different interpretation of the same facts that seems better than the first, that person will swing away from the first argument, thinking he or she has found "stronger facts."

However, if that person had been helped to understand this issue of presuppositions, then he or she would have been better able to recognize this for what it is—a different interpretation based on differing presuppositions (i.e., starting beliefs).

Debate terms

Often people who don't believe the Bible will say that they aren't interested in hearing about the Bible. They want real proof that there's a God who created. They'll listen to our claims about Christianity, but they want proof without mentioning the Bible.

If one agrees to a discussion without using the Bible as these people insist, then we have allowed them to set the terms of the debate. In essence these terms are

1. "Facts" are neutral. However, there are no such things as "brute facts"; all facts are interpreted. Once the Bible is eliminated from the argument, the Christians' presuppositions are gone, leaving them unable to effectively give an alternate interpretation of the facts. Their opponents then have the upper hand as they still have their presuppositions.

2. Truth can/should be determined independently of God. However, the Bible states: "The fear of the Lord is the beginning of wisdom" (Psalm 111:10); "The fear of the Lord is the beginning of knowledge" (Proverbs 1:7); "But the natural man does not receive the things of the Spirit of God, for they are foolishness to him; neither can he know them, because they are spiritually discerned" (1 Corinthians 2:14).

A Christian cannot divorce the spiritual nature of the battle from the battle itself. A non-Christian is not neutral. The Bible makes this very clear: "The one who is not with Me is against

Me, and the one who does not gather with Me scatters" (Matthew 12:30); "And this is the condemnation, that the Light has come into the world, and men loved darkness rather than the Light, because their deeds were evil" (John 3:19).

Agreeing to such terms of debate also implicitly accepts the proposition that the Bible's account of the universe's history is irrelevant to understanding that history!

Ultimately, God's Word convicts

First Peter 3:15 and other passages make it clear we are to use every argument we can to convince people of the truth, and 2 Corinthians 10:4–5 says we are to refute error (as Paul did in his ministry to the Gentiles). Nonetheless, we must never forget Hebrews 4:12: "For the word of God is living and powerful and sharper than any two-edged sword, piercing even to the dividing apart of soul and spirit, and of the joints and marrow, and is a discerner of the thoughts and intents of the heart."

Also, Isaiah 55:11 says, "So shall My word be, which goes out of My mouth; it shall not return to Me void, but it shall accomplish what I please, and it shall certainly do what I sent it to do."

Even though our human arguments may be powerful, ultimately it is God's Word that convicts and opens people to the truth. In all of our arguments, we must not divorce what we are saying from the Word that convicts.

Practical application

When someone says he wants "proof" or "evidence," not the Bible, one might respond as follows:

> You might not believe the Bible, but I do. And I believe it gives me the right basis to understand this universe and correctly interpret the facts around me. I'm going to give you some examples of how building my thinking on

the Bible explains the world and is not contradicted by science.

One can, of course, do this with numerous scientific examples, showing, for example, how the issue of sin and judgment is relevant to geology and fossil evidence; how the fall of man, with the subsequent curse on creation, makes sense of the evidence of harmful mutations, violence, and death; or how the original "kinds" of animals gave rise to the wide variety of animals we see today.

Choose a topic and develop it:

For instance, the Bible states that God made distinct kinds of animals and plants. Let me show you what happens when I build my thinking on this presupposition. I will illustrate how processes such as natural selection, genetic drift, etc., can be explained and interpreted. You will see how the science of genetics makes sense based upon the Bible. Evolutionists believe in natural selection—that is real science, as you observe it happening. Well, creationists also believe in natural selection. Evolutionists accept the science of genetics—well, so do creationists.

However, here is the difference: evolutionists believe that, over millions of years, one kind of animal has changed into a totally different kind. However, creationists, based on the Bible's account of origins, believe that God created separate kinds of animals and plants to reproduce their own kind; therefore, one kind will not turn into a totally different kind.

Now this can be tested in the present. The scientific observations support the creationist interpretation that the changes we see are not creating new information. The changes are all within the originally created pool of information of that kind—sorting, shuffling, or degrading it. The creationist account of history, based on the Bible, provides the correct basis to interpret the facts of the present; and real science confirms the interpretation.

After this detailed explanation, continue like this:

Now let me ask you to defend your position concerning these matters. Please show me how your way of thinking, based on your beliefs, makes sense of the same evidence. And I want you to point out where my science and logic are wrong.

In arguing this way, a Christian is

1. using biblical presuppositions to build a way of thinking to interpret the evidence;

2. showing that the Bible and science go hand in hand;

3. challenging the presuppositions of the other person (many are unaware they have these);

4. forcing the debater to logically defend his position consistent with science and his own presuppositions (many will find that they cannot do this), and help this person realize they do have presuppositions that can be challenged;

5. honoring the Word of God that convicts the soul.

If Christians really understood that all facts are actually interpreted on the basis of certain presuppositions, we wouldn't be in the least bit intimidated by the evolutionists' supposed "evidence." We should instead be looking at the evolutionists' (or old-earthers'[1]) interpretation of the evidence, and how the same evidence could be interpreted within a biblical framework and confirmed by testable and repeatable science. If more creationists did this, they would be less likely to jump at flaky evidence that seems startling but in reality has been interpreted incorrectly in their rush to find the knockdown, drag-out convincing "evidence" against evolution that they think they desperately need.

The various age-dating methods are also subject to interpretation. All dating methods suffer, in principle, from the same limitations—whether they are used to support a young world or an old world. For instance, the public reads almost daily in newspapers and magazines that scientists have dated a particular rock at billions of years old. Most just accept this. However, creation scientists have learned to ask questions as to how this date was obtained—what method was used and what assumptions were accepted to develop this method? These scientists then question those assumptions (questions) to see whether they are valid and to determine whether the rock's age could be interpreted differently. Then the results are published to help people understand that scientists have not proven that the rock is billions of years old and that the facts can be interpreted in a different way to support a young age.

Consider the research from the creationist group Radioisotopes and the Age of The Earth (RATE) concerning the age of zircon crystals in granite.[2] Using one set of assumptions, these crystals could be interpreted to be around 1.5 billion years old, based on the amount of lead produced from the decay of uranium (which also produces helium). However, if one questions these assumptions, one is motivated to test them. Measurements of the rate at which helium is able to "leak out" of these crystals indicate that if they were much older than about 6,000 years, they would have nowhere near the amount of helium still left in them. Hence, the originally applied assumption of a constant decay rate is flawed; one must assume, instead, that there has been acceleration of the decay rate in the past. Using this revised assumption, the same uranium-lead data can now be interpreted to also give an age of fewer than 6,000 years.

Another example involves red blood cells and traces of hemoglobin that have been found in T. rex bones, although these should have long decomposed if they were millions of years old. Yet the reaction of the researchers was a perfect illustration of how evolutionary bias can result in trying to explain away hard facts to fit the preconceived framework of millions of years:

It was exactly like looking at a slice of modern bone. But, of course, I couldn't believe it. I said to the lab technician: "The bones, after all, are 65 million years old. How could blood cells survive that long?"[3]

Whenever you hear a news report that scientists have found another "missing link" or discovered a fossil "millions of years old," try to think about the right questions that need to be asked to challenge the questions these scientists asked to get their interpretations!

All of this should be a lesson for us to take note of the situation when we read the newspaper—we are reading someone's interpretation of the facts of world history—there very well could be a different way of looking at the same "facts." One can see this in practice on television when comparing a news network that's currently considered fairly liberal (CNN) with one that is more conservative (FOX)—one can often see the same "facts" interpreted differently!

The reason so many Christian professors (and Christian leaders in general) have rejected the literal creation position is that they have blindly accepted the interpretation of facts from the secular world, based on man's fallible presuppositions about history. And they have then tried to reinterpret the Bible accordingly. If only they would start with the presupposition that God's Word is true, they would find that they could then correctly interpret the facts of the present and show overwhelmingly that observational science repeatedly confirms such interpretations.

Don't forget, as Christians we need to always build our thinking on the Word of the One who has the answers to all of the questions that could ever be asked—the infinite Creator God. He has revealed the true history of the universe in His Word to enable us to develop the right way of thinking about the present and thus determine the correct interpretations of the evidence of the present. We should follow Proverbs 1:7 and 9:10, which teach that fear of the Lord is the beginning of true wisdom and knowledge.

The bottom line

The bottom line is that it's not a matter of who has the better (or the most) "facts on their side." We need to understand that there are no such things as brute facts—all facts are interpreted. The next time evolutionists use what seem to be convincing facts for evolution, try to determine the presuppositions they have used to interpret these facts. Then, beginning with the big picture of history from the Bible, look at the same facts through these biblical glasses and interpret them differently. Next, using the real science of the present that an evolutionist also uses, see if that science, when properly understood, confirms (by being consistent with) the interpretation based on the Bible. You will find over and over again that the Bible is confirmed by real science.

But remember that, like Job, we need to understand that compared to God we know next to nothing (Job 42:2–6). We won't have all the answers. However, so many answers have come to light now that a Christian can give a credible defense of the Book of Genesis and show it is the correct foundation for thinking about, and interpreting, every aspect of reality.

Therefore, let's not jump in a blind-faith way at the startling facts we think we need to "prove" creation—trying to counter "their facts" with "our facts." (Jesus himself rose from the dead in the most startling possible demonstration of the truth of God's Word. But many still wouldn't believe—see Luke 16:27–31.) Instead, let's not let apparent facts for evolution intimidate us, but let's understand the right way to think about facts. We can then deal with the same facts the evolutionists use, to show they have the wrong framework of interpretation—and that the facts of the real world really do conform to, and confirm, the Bible. In this way we can do battle for a biblical worldview.

Remember, it's no good convincing people to believe in creation, without also leading them to believe and trust in the Creator and Redeemer, Jesus Christ. God honors those who honor

His Word. We need to use God-honoring ways of reaching people with the truth of what life is all about.

1. Those who accept millions of years of history.

2. R. Humphreys et al., "Helium Diffusion Rates Support Accelerated Nuclear Decay," www.icr.org/pdf/research/Helium_ICC_7-22-03.pdf.

3. *Science* 261 (July 9, 1994): 160; see also, "Scientists Recover T. rex Soft Tissue: 70-mil-lionyear- old Fossil Yields Preserved Blood Vessels," www.msnbc.msn.com/id/7285683/, March 24, 2005.

Ken Ham, President and CEO, Answers in Genesis–USA & the Creation Museum

Ken's bachelor's degree in applied science (with an emphasis on environmental biology) was awarded by the Queensland Institute of Technology in Australia. He also holds a diploma of education from the University of Queensland. In recognition of the contribution Ken has made to the church in the USA and internationally, Ken has been awarded two honorary doctorates: a Doctor of Divinity (1997) from Temple Baptist College in Cincinnati, Ohio and a Doctor of Literature (2004) from Liberty University in Lynchburg, Virginia.

Since moving to America in 1987, Ken has become one of the most in-demand Christian conference speakers and talk show guests in America. He has appeared on national shows such as Fox's *The O'Reilly Factor* and *Fox and Friends in the Morning*; CNN's *The Situation Room with Wolf Blitzer*, ABC's *Good Morning America*, the BBC, *CBS News Sunday Morning*, *The NBC Nightly News with Brian Williams*, and *The PBS News Hour with Jim Lehrer*.

10 Best Evidences from Science that Confirm a Young Earth

by Andrew Snelling, David Menton, Danny Faulkner, and Georgia Purdom

The earth is only a few thousand years old. That's a fact, plainly revealed in God's Word. So we should expect to find plenty of evidence for its youth. And that's what we find—in the earth's geology, biology, paleontology, and even astronomy.

Literally hundreds of dating methods could be used to attempt an estimate of the earth's age, and the vast majority of them point to a much younger earth than the 4.5 billion years claimed by secularists. The following presents what Answers in Genesis researchers picked as the ten best scientific evidences that contradict billions of years and confirm a relatively young earth and universe.

Despite this wealth of evidence, it is important to understand that, from the perspective of observational science, no one can prove absolutely how young (or old) the universe is. Only one dating method is absolutely reliable—a witness who doesn't lie, who has all evidence, and who can reveal to us when the universe began!

And we do have such a witness—the God of the Bible! He has given us a specific history, beginning with the six days of creation and followed by detailed genealogies that allow us to determine when the universe began. Based on this history, the beginning was only about six thousand years ago (about four thousand years from Creation to Christ).

In the rush to examine all these amazing scientific "evidences," it's easy to lose sight of the big picture. Such a mountain of scientific evidence, accumulated by researchers, seems to obviously contradict the supposed billions of years, so why don't more people rush to accept the truth of a young earth based on the Bible?

The problem is, as we consider the topic of origins, all so-called "evidences" must be interpreted. Facts don't speak for themselves. Interpreting the facts of the present becomes especially difficult when reconstructing the historical events that produced those present-day facts, because no humans have always been present to observe all the evidence and to record how all the evidence was produced.

Forensic scientists must make multiple assumptions about things they cannot observe. How was the original setting different? Were different processes in play? Was the scene later contaminated? Just one wrong assumption or one tiny piece of missing evidence could totally change how they reconstruct the past events that led to the present-day evidence.

That's why, when discussing the age of the earth, Christians must be ready to explain the importance of starting points and assumptions. Reaching the correct conclusions requires the right starting point.

The Bible is that starting point. This is the revealed Word of the almighty, faithful, and true Creator, who was present to observe all events of earth history and who gave mankind an infallible record of key events in the past.

The Bible, God's revelation to us, gives us the foundation that enables us to begin to build the right worldview to correctly understand how the present and past are connected. All other documents written by man are fallible, unlike the "God-breathed" infallible Word (2 Timothy 3:16). The Bible clearly and unmistakably describes the creation of the universe, the solar system, and the earth around six thousand years ago. We know that it's true based on the authority of God's own character. "Because He could swear by no one greater, He swore by Himself" (Hebrews 6:13).

In one sense, God's testimony is all we need; but God Himself tells us to give reasons for what we believe (1 Peter 3:15). So it is also important to conduct scientific research (that is part of taking dominion of the earth, as Adam was told to do in Genesis 1:28). With this research we can challenge those who reject God's clear Word and defend the biblical worldview.

Indeed, God's testimony must have such a central role in our thinking that it seems demeaning even to call it the "best" evidence of a young earth. It is, in truth, the only foundation upon which all other evidences can be correctly understood!

#1 Very little sediment on the seafloor

If sediments have been accumulating on the seafloor for three billion years, the seafloor should be choked with sediments many miles deep.

Every year water and wind erode about 20 billion tons of dirt and rock debris from the continents and deposit them on the seafloor.[1] (Figure 1). Most of this material accumulates as loose sediments near the continents. Yet the average thickness of all these sediments globally over the whole seafloor is not even 1,300 feet (400 m).[2]

Some sediments appear to be removed as tectonic plates slide slowly (an inch or two per year) beneath continents. An estimated 1 billion tons of sediments are removed this way each year.[2] The net gain is thus 19 billion tons per year. At this rate, 1,300 feet of sediment would accumulate in less than 12 million years, not billions of years.

This evidence makes sense within the context of the Genesis Flood cataclysm, not the idea of slow and gradual geologic evolution. In the latter stages of the year-long global Flood, water swiftly drained off the emerging land, dumping its sediment-chocked loads offshore. Thus most seafloor sediments accumulated rapidly about 4,300 years ago.[3]

Where is all the sediment?

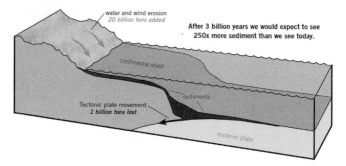

Figure 1: Every year, 20 billion tons of dirt and rock debris wash into the ocean and accumulate on the seafloor. Only 1 billion tons (5%) are removed by tectonic plates. At this rate, the current thickness of seafloor sediment would accumulate in less than 12 million years. Such sediments are easily explained by water draining off the continents towards the end of the Flood.

Rescuing devices

Those who advocate an old earth insist that the seafloor sediments must have accumulated at a much slower rate in the past. But this rescuing device doesn't "stack up"! Like the sediment layers on the continents, the sediments on the continental shelves and margins (the majority of the seafloor sediments) have features that unequivocally indicate they were deposited much faster than today's rates. For example, the layering and patterns of various grain sizes in these sediments are the same as those produced by undersea landslides, when dense debris-laden currents (called turbidity currents) flow rapidly across the continental shelves and the sediments then settle in thick layers over vast areas. An additional problem for the old-earth view is that no evidence exists of much sediment being subducted and mixed into the mantle.

#2 Bent rock layers

In many mountainous areas, rock layers thousands of feet thick have been bent and folded without fracturing. How can that happen if they were laid down separately over hundreds of millions of years and already hardened?

If the earth's fossil-bearing sedimentary layers were laid down over 460 million years, they could not be bent without breaking.

Hardened rock layers are brittle. Try bending a slab of concrete sometime to see what happens! But if concrete is still wet, it can easily be shaped and molded before the cement sets. The same principle applies to sedimentary rock layers. They can be bent and folded soon after the sediment is deposited, before the natural cements have a chance to bind the particles together into hard, brittle rocks.[4]

The region around Grand Canyon is a great example showing how most of the earth's fossil-bearing layers were laid down quickly and many were folded while still wet. Exposed in the canyon's walls are about 4,500 feet (1,370 meters) of fossil-bearing layers, conventionally labelled Cambrian to Permian.[5] They were supposedly deposited over a period lasting from 520 to 250 million years ago. Then, amazingly, this whole sequence of layers rose over a mile, around 60 million years ago. The plateau through which Grand Canyon runs is now 7,000–8,000 feet (2,150–3,450 meters) above sea level.

Layers laid down quickly and bent while soft

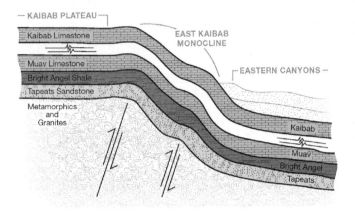

Figure 2: The Grand Canyon now cuts through many rock layers. Previously, all these layers were raised to their current elevation (a raised, flat region known as the Kaibab Plateau). Somehow this whole sequence was bent and folded without fracturing. That's impossible if the first layer, the Tapeats Sandstone, was deposited over North America 460 million years before being folded. But all the layers would still be relatively soft and pliable if it all happened during the recent, global Flood.

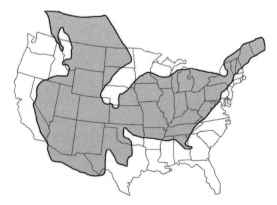

Figure 3: This phenomenon was not regional. The Tapeats Sandstone spans the continent, and other layers span much of the globe.

Think about it. The time between the first deposits at Grand Canyon (520 million years ago) and their bending (60 million years ago) was 460 million years!

Look at the photos of some of these layers at the edge of the plateau, just east of the Grand Canyon. The whole sequence of these hardened sedimentary rock layers has been bent and folded, but without fracturing (Figure 2).[6] At the bottom of this sequence is the Tapeats Sandstone, which is 100–325 feet (30–100 meters) thick. It is bent and folded 90° (Photo 1). The Muav Limestone above it has similarly been bent (Photo 2).

Photo 1: The whole sequence of sedimentary layers through which Grand Canyon cuts has been bent and folded without fracturing. This includes the Tapeats Sandstone, located at the bottom of the sequence. (A 90° fold in the eastern Grand Canyon is pictured here.) Photo courtesy Andrew A. Snelling

Photo 2: All the layers through which Grand Canyon cuts—including the Muav Limestone shown here—have been bent without fracturing. Photo courtesy Andrew A. Snelling

However, it supposedly took 270 million years to deposit these particular layers. Surely in that time the Tapeats Sandstone at the bottom would have dried out and the sand grains cemented together, especially with 4,000 feet (1,220 m) of rock layers piled on top of it and pressing down on it? The only viable scientific explanation is that the whole sequence was deposited very quickly—the creation model indicates that it took less than a year, during the global Flood cataclysm. So the 520 million years never happened, and the earth is young.

Rescuing devices

What solution do old-earth advocates suggest? Heat and pressure can make hard rock layers pliable, so they claim this must be what happened in the eastern Grand Canyon, as the sequence of many layers above pressed down and heated up these rocks. Just one problem. The heat and pressure would have transformed these layers into quartzite, marble, and other metamorphic rocks. Yet Tapeats Sandstone is still sandstone, a sedimentary rock!

But this quandary is even worse for those who deny God's recent creation and the Flood. The Tapeats Sandstone and its equivalents can be traced right across North America (Figure 3),[7] and beyond to right across northern Africa to southern Israel.[8] Indeed, the whole Grand Canyon sedimentary sequence is an integral part of six megasequences that cover North America.[9] Only a global Flood cataclysm could carry the sediments to deposit thick layers across several continents one after the other in rapid succession in one event.[10]

#3 Soft tissue in fossils

Ask the average layperson how he or she knows that the earth is millions or billions of years old, and that person will probably mention the dinosaurs, which nearly everybody "knows" died off 65 million years ago. A recent discovery by Dr. Mary Schweitzer, however, has given reason for all but committed evolutionists to question this assumption.

If dinosaurs lived over 65 million years ago, why do some dinosaur fossils still contain well-preserved soft tissues?

Bone slices from the fossilized thigh bone (femur) of a *Tyrannosaurus rex* found in the Hell Creek formation of Montana were studied under the microscope by Schweitzer. To her amazement, the bone showed what appeared to be blood vessels of the type seen in bone and marrow, and these contained what appeared to be red blood cells with nuclei, typical of reptiles and birds (but not mammals). The vessels even appeared to be lined with specialized endothelial cells found in all blood vessels.

Amazingly, the bone marrow contained what appeared to be flexible tissue. Initially, some skeptical scientists suggested that bacterial biofilms (dead bacteria aggregated in a slime) formed what only appear to be blood vessels and bone cells. Recently Schweitzer and coworkers found biochemical evidence for intact fragments of the protein collagen, which is the building block of connective tissue. This is important because collagen is a highly distinctive protein not made by bacteria. (See Schweitzer's review article in *Scientific American* [December 2010, pp. 62–69] titled "Blood from Stone.")

Some evolutionists have strongly criticized Schweitzer's conclusions because they are understandably reluctant to concede the existence of blood vessels, cells with nuclei, tissue elasticity, and intact protein fragments in a dinosaur bone dated at 68 million years old. Other evolutionists, who find Schweitzer's evidence too compelling to ignore, simply conclude that there is some previously unrecognized form of fossilization that preserves cells and protein fragments over tens of millions of years.[11] Needless to say, no evolutionist has publicly considered the possibility that dinosaur fossils are not millions of years old.

A largely intact dinosaur mummy, named Dakota, was found in the Hell Creek Formation of the Western U.S. in 2007. Some soft tissue from the long-necked hadrosaur was quickly preserved as fossil, such as the scales from its forearm shown here. Photo: Tyler Lyson, Associated Press

An obvious question arises from Schweitzer's work: is it even remotely plausible that blood vessels, cells, and protein fragments can exist largely intact over 68 million years? While many consider such long-term preservation of tissue and cells to be very unlikely, the problem is that no human or animal remains are known with certainty to be 68 million years old. But if creationists are right, dinosaurs died off only 3,000–4,000 years ago. So would we expect the preservation of vessels, cells, and complex molecules of the type that Schweitzer reports for biological tissues historically known to be 3,000–4,000 years old?

The answer is yes. Many studies of Egyptian mummies and other humans of this old age (confirmed by historical evidence) show all the sorts of detail Schweitzer reported in her *T. rex*. In addition to Egyptian mummies, the Tyrolean iceman, found in the Alps in 1991 and believed to be about 5,000 years old, shows such incredible preservation of DNA and other microscopic detail.

We conclude that the preservation of vessels, cells, and complex molecules in dinosaurs is entirely consistent with a young-earth creationist perspective but is highly implausible with the evolutionist's perspective about dinosaurs that died off millions of years ago.

#4 Faint sun paradox

Evidence now supports astronomers' belief that the sun's power comes from the fusion of hydrogen into helium deep in the sun's core, but there is a huge problem. As the hydrogen fuses, it should change the composition of the sun's core, gradually increasing the sun's temperature. If true, this means that the earth was colder in the past. In fact, the earth would have been below freezing 3.5 billion years ago, when life supposedly evolved.

The rate of nuclear fusion depends upon the temperature. As the sun's core temperatures increase, the sun's energy output should also increase, causing the sun to brighten over time. Calculations show that the sun would brighten by 25% after 3.5 billion years. This means that an early sun would have been fainter, with the average temperature on the early earth 31°F (17C) less than it is today. The average temperature then would have been 28°F (-2C). That's below freezing!

But evolutionists acknowledge that there is no evidence of this in the geologic record. They even call this problem the faint young sun paradox. While this isn't a problem over many thousands of years, it is a problem if the world is billions of years old.

Rescuing devices

Over the years scientists have proposed several mechanisms to explain away this problem. These suggestions require changes in the earth's atmosphere. For instance, more greenhouse gases early in earth's history would retain more heat, but this means that the greenhouse gases had to decrease gradually to compensate for the brightening sun.

None of these proposals can be proved, for there is no evidence. Furthermore, it is difficult to believe that a mechanism totally unrelated to the sun's brightness could compensate for the sun's changing emission so precisely for billions of years.

#5 Rapidly decaying magnetic field

The earth is surrounded by a magnetic field that protects living things from solar radiation. Without it, life could not exist. That's why scientists were surprised to discover that the field is quickly wearing down. At the current rate, the field and thus the earth could be no older than 20,000 years old.

The earth's magnetic field is wearing down so quickly that it could be no more than 20,000 years old.

Several measurements confirm this decay. Since measuring began in 1845, the total energy stored in the earth's magnetic field has been decaying at a rate of 5% per century.[12] Archaeological measurements show that the field was 40% stronger in AD 1000.[13] Recent records of the International Geomagnetic Reference Field, the most accurate ever taken, show a net energy loss of 1.4% in just three decades (1970–2000)[14] This means that the field's energy has halved every 1,465 years or so.

Creationists have proposed that the earth's magnetic field is caused by a freely-decaying electric current in the earth's core. This means that the electric current naturally loses energy, or "decays," as it flows through the metallic core. Though it differs from the most commonly accepted conventional model, it is consistent with our knowledge of what makes up the earth's core.[15] Furthermore, based on what we know about the conductive properties of liquid iron, this freely decaying current would have started when the earth's outer core was formed. However, if the core were more than 20,000 years old, then the starting energy would have made the earth too hot to be covered by water, as Genesis 1:2 reveals.

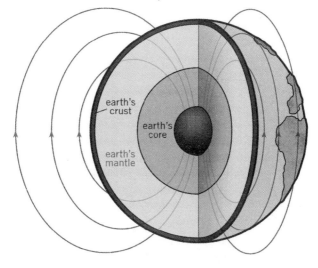

Figure 4: Creationists have proposed that the earth's magnetic field is caused by a freely decaying electric current in the earth's core. (Old-earth scientists are forced to adopt a theoretical, self-sustaining process known as the dynamo model, which contradicts some basic laws of physics.) Reliable, accurate, published geological field data have emphatically confirmed this young-earth model.

Reliable, accurate, published geological field data have emphatically confirmed the young-earth model: a freely-decaying electric current in the outer core is generating the magnetic field.[16] Although this field reversed direction several times during the Flood cataclysm when the outer core was stirred (Figure 4), the field has rapidly and continuously lost total energy ever since creation (Figure 5). It all points to an earth and magnetic field only about 6,000 years old.[17]

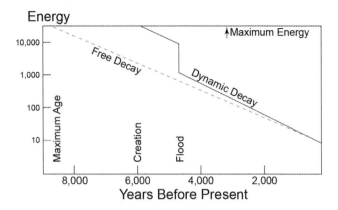

Figure 5: The earth's magnetic field has rapidly and continuously lost total energy since its origin, no matter which model has been adopted to explain its magnetism. According to creationists' dynamic decay model, the earth's magnetic field lost more energy during the Flood, when the outer core was stirred and the field reversed direction several times.

Rescuing devices

Old-earth advocates maintain the earth is over 4.5 billion years old, so they believe the magnetic field must be self-sustaining. They propose a complex, theoretical process known as the dynamo model, but such a model contradicts some basic laws of physics. Furthermore, their model fails to explain the modern, measured electric current in the seafloor.[18] Nor can it explain the past field reversals, computer simulations notwithstanding.[19]

To salvage their old earth and dynamo, some have suggested the magnetic field decay is linear rather than exponential, in spite of the historic measurements and decades of experiments confirming the exponential decay. Others have suggested that the strength of some components increases to make up for other components that are decaying. That claim results from confusion about the difference between magnetic field intensity and its energy, and has been refuted categorically by creation physicists.[20]

#6 Helium in radioactive rocks

During the radioactive decay of uranium and thorium contained in rocks, lots of helium is produced. Because helium is the second lightest element and a noble gas—meaning it does not combine with other atoms—it readily diffuses (leaks) out and eventually escapes into the atmosphere. Helium diffuses so rapidly that all the helium should have leaked out in less than 100,000 years. So why are these rocks still full of helium atoms?

While drilling deep Precambrian (pre-Flood) granitic rocks in New Mexico, geologists extracted samples of zircon (zirconium silicate) crystals from different depths. The crystals contained not only uranium but also large amounts of helium.[21] The hotter the rocks, the faster the helium should escape, so researchers were surprised to find that the deepest, and therefore hottest, zircons (at 387°F or 197C) contained far more helium than expected. Up to 58% of the helium that the uranium could have ever generated was still present in the crystals.

The helium leakage rate has been determined in several experiments.[22] All measurements are in agreement. Helium diffuses so rapidly that all the helium in these zircon crystals should have leaked out in less than 100,000 years. The fact that so much helium is still there means they cannot be 1.5 billion years old, as uranium-lead dating suggests. Indeed, using the measured rate of helium diffusion, these pre-Flood rocks have an average "diffusion age" of only 6,000 (± 2,000) years.[23]

These experimentally determined and repeatable results, based on the well-understood physical process of diffusion, thus emphatically demonstrate that these zircons are only a few thousand years old. The supposed 1.5-billion-year age is based on the unverifiable assumptions of radioisotope dating that are radically wrong.[24]

Another evidence of a young earth is the low amount of helium in the atmosphere. The leakage rate of helium gas into the atmosphere has been measured.[25] Even though some helium escapes into outer space, the amount still present is not nearly enough if the earth is over 4.5 billion years old.[26] In fact, if we assume no helium was in the original atmosphere, all the helium would have accumulated in only 1.8 million years even from an evolutionary standpoint.[27] But when the catastrophic Flood upheaval is factored in, which rapidly released huge amounts of helium into the atmosphere, it could have accumulated in only 6,000 years.[28]

Rescuing devices

So glaring and devastating is the surprisingly large amount of helium that old-earth advocates have attempted to discredit this evidence.

One critic suggested the helium didn't all come from uranium decay in the zircon crystals but a lot diffused into them from the surrounding minerals. But this proposal ignores measurements showing that less helium gas is in the surrounding minerals. Due to the well-established diffusion law of physics, gases always diffuse from areas of higher concentration to surrounding areas of lower concentration.[29]

Another critic suggested the edges of the zircon crystals must have stopped the helium from leaking out, effectively "bottling" the helium within the zircons. However, this postulation has also been easily refuted because the zircon crystals are wedged between flat mica sheets, not wrapped in them, so that helium could easily flow between the sheets unrestricted.[30] All other critics have been answered.[31] Thus all available evidence confirms that the true age of these zircons and their host granitic rock is only 6,000 (± 2,000) years.

Helium in radioactive rocks: quick escape of helium

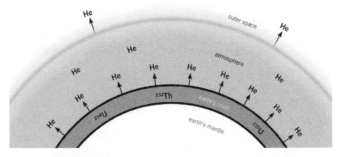

Figure 6: Radioactive elements in rocks produce a lot of helium as they decay; and this gas quickly slips away into the atmosphere, especially when the rocks are hot. Yet radioactive rocks in the earth's crust contain a lot of helium. The only possible explanation: the helium hasn't had time to escape!

#7 Carbon-14 in fossils, coal, and diamonds

Carbon-14 (or radiocarbon) is a radioactive form of carbon that scientists use to date fossils. But it decays so quickly—with a half-life of only 5,730 years—that none is expected to remain in fossils after only a few hundred thousand years. Yet carbon-14 has been detected in "ancient" fossils—supposedly up to hundreds of millions of years old—ever since the earliest days of radiocarbon dating.[32]

If radiocarbon lasts only a few hundred thousand years, why is it found in all the earth's diamonds dated at billions of years old?

Even if every atom in the whole earth were carbon-14, they would decay so quickly that no carbon-14 would be left on earth after only 1 million years. Contrary to expectations, between 1984 and 1998 alone, the scientific literature reported carbon-14 in 70 samples that came from fossils, coal, oil, natural gas, and marble representing the fossil-bearing portion of the geologic record, supposedly spanning more than 500 million years. All contained radiocarbon.[33] Further, analyses of fossilized wood and coal samples, supposedly spanning 32–350 million years in age, yielded ages between 20,000 and 50,000 years using carbon-14 dating.[34] Diamonds supposedly 1–3 billion years old similarly yielded carbon-14 ages of only 55,000 years.[35]

A sea creature, called an ammonite, was discovered near Redding, California, accompanied by fossilized wood. Both fossils are claimed by strata dating to be 112–120 million years old but yielded radiocarbon ages of only thousands of years.

Even that is too old when you realize that these ages assume that the earth's magnetic field has always been constant. But it was stronger in the past, protecting the atmosphere from solar radiation and reducing the radiocarbon production. As a result, past creatures had much less radiocarbon in their bodies, and their deaths occurred much more recently than reported!

So the radiocarbon ages of all fossils and coal should be reduced to less than 5,000 years, matching the timing of their burial during the Flood. The age of diamonds should be reduced to the approximate time of biblical creation—about 6,000 years ago.[36]

Rescuing devices

Old-earth advocates repeat the same two hackneyed defenses, even though they were resoundingly demolished years ago. The first cry is, "It's all contamination." Yet for thirty years AMS radiocarbon laboratories have subjected all samples, before they carbon-14 date them, to repeated brutal treatments with strong acids and bleaches to rid them of all contamination.[37] And when the instruments are tested with blank samples, they yield zero radiocarbon, so there can't be any contamination or instrument problems.

The second cry is, "New radiocarbon was formed directly in the fossils when nearby decaying uranium bombarded traces of nitrogen in the buried fossils." Carbon-14 does form from such transformation of nitrogen, but actual calculations demonstrate conclusively this process does not produce the levels of radiocarbon that world-class laboratories have found in fossils, coal, and diamonds.[38]

#8 Short-lived comets

A comet spends most of its time far from the sun in the deep freeze of space. But once each orbit a comet comes very close to the sun, allowing the sun's heat to evaporate much of the comet's ice and dislodge dust to form a beautiful tail. Comets have little mass, so each close pass to the sun greatly reduces a comet's size, and eventually comets fade away. They can't survive billions of years.

Two other mechanisms can destroy comets—ejections from the solar system and collisions with planets. Ejections happen as comets pass too close to the large planets, particularly Jupiter, and the planets' gravity kicks them out of the solar system. While ejections have been observed many times, the first observed collision was in 1994, when Comet Shoemaker-Levi IX slammed into Jupiter.

Given the loss rates, it's easy to compute a maximum age of comets. That maximum age is only a few million years. Obviously, their prevalence makes sense if the entire solar system was created just a few thousand years ago, but not if it arose billions of years ago.

Rescuing devices

Evolutionary astronomers have answered this problem by claiming that comets must come from two sources. They propose that a Kuiper belt beyond the orbit of Neptune hosts short-period comets (comets with orbits under 200 years), and a much larger, distant Oort cloud hosts long-period comets (comets with orbits over 200 years).

Yet there is no evidence for the supposed Oort cloud, and there likely never will be. In the past twenty years astronomers have found thousands of asteroids orbiting beyond Neptune, and they are assumed to be the Kuiper belt. However, the large size of these asteroids (Pluto is one of the larger ones) and the difference in composition between these asteroids and comets argue against this conclusion.

#9 Very little salt in the sea

If the world's oceans have been around for three billion years as evolutionists believe, they should be filled with vastly more salt than the oceans contain today.

After 3 billion years, we would expect to see 70x more salt in the ocean than we see today.

Every year rivers, glaciers, underground seepage, and atmospheric and volcanic dust dump large amounts of salts into the oceans (Figure 7). Consider the influx of the predominant salt, sodium chloride (common table salt). Some 458 million tons of sodium mixes into ocean water each year,[39] but only 122 million tons (27%) is removed by other natural processes[40] (Figure 7).

If seawater originally contained no sodium (salt) and the sodium accumulated at today's rates, then today's ocean saltiness would be reached in only 42 million years[41]—only about 1/70 the three billion years evolutionists propose. But those assumptions fail to take into account the likelihood that God created a saltwater ocean for all the sea creatures He made on Day Five. Also, the year-long global Flood cataclysm must have dumped an unprecedented amount of salt into the ocean through erosion, sedimentation, and volcanism. So today's ocean saltiness makes much better sense within the biblical timescale of about six thousand years.[42]

Salt in the sea: the numbers just don't add up

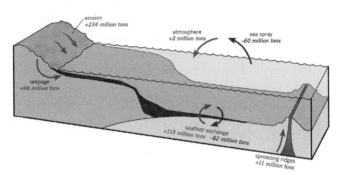

Figure 7: Every year, the continents, atmosphere, and seafloor add 458 million tons of salt into the ocean, but only 122 million tons (27%) is removed. At this rate, today's saltiness would be reached in 42 million years. But God originally created a salty ocean for sea creatures, and the Flood quickly added more salt.

Rescuing devices

Those who believe in a three-billion-year-old ocean say that past sodium inputs had to be less and outputs greater. However, even the most generous estimates can only stretch the accumulation timeframe to 62 million years.[43] Long-agers also argue that huge amounts of sodium are removed during the formation of basalts at mid-ocean ridges,[44] but this ignores the fact that the sodium returns to the ocean as seafloor basalts move away from the ridges.[45]

#10 DNA in "ancient" bacteria

In 2000, scientists claimed to have "resurrected" bacteria, named Lazarus bacteria, discovered in a salt crystal conventionally dated at 250 million years old. They were shocked that the bacteria's DNA was very similar to modern bacterial DNA. If the modern bacteria were the result of 250 million years of evolution, its DNA should be very different from the Lazarus bacteria (based on known mutation rates).

In addition, the scientists were surprised to find that the DNA was still intact after the supposed 250 million years. DNA normally breaks down quickly, even in ideal conditions. Even evolutionists agree that DNA in bacterial spores (a dormant state) should not last more than a million years. Their quandary is quite substantial.

However, the discovery of Lazarus bacteria is not shocking or surprising when we base our expectations on the Bible accounts. For instance, Noah's Flood likely deposited the salt beds that were home to the bacteria. If the Lazarus bacteria are only about 4,500 years old (the approximate number of years that have passed since the worldwide flood), their DNA is more likely to be intact and similar to modern bacteria.

Rescuing devices

Some scientists have dismissed the finding and believe the Lazarus bacteria are contamination from modern bacteria. But the scientists who discovered the bacteria defend the rigorous procedures used to avoid contamination. They claim the old age is valid if the bacteria had longer generation times, different mutation rates, and/or similar selection pressures compared to modern bacteria. Of course these "rescuing devices" are only conjectures to make the data fit their worldview.

---

1.   John D. Milliman and James P. N. Syvitski, "Geomorphic/Tectonic Control of Sediment Discharge to the Ocean: The Importance of Small Mountainous Rivers," *The Journal of Geology* 100 (1992): 525–544.

2.   William W. Hay, James L. Sloan II, and Christopher N. Wold, "Mass/Age Distribution and Composition of Sediments on the Ocean Floor and the Global Rate of Sediment Subduction," *Journal of Geophysical Research* 93, no. B12 (1998): 14,933–14,940.

---

3.   For a fuller treatment and further information see: John D. Morris, *The Young Earth* (Green Forest, AR: Master Books, 2000), pp. 88–90. Andrew A. Snelling, *Earth's Catastrophic Past: Geology, Creation and the Flood* (Dallas, TX: Institute for Creation Research, 2009), pp. 881–884.

4.   R.E. Goodman, *Introduction to Rock Mechanics* (New York: John Wiley and Sons, 1980); Sam Boggs, Jr., *Principles of Sedimentology and Stratigraphy* (Upper Saddle River, NJ: Prentice-Hall, 1995), pp. 127–131.

5.   Stanley S. Beus and Michael Morales, eds., *Grand Canyon Geology*, 2nd edition (New York: Oxford University Press, 2003).

6.   Andrew A. Snelling, "Rock Layers Folded, Not Fractured," *Answers* 4, no. 2 (April–June 2009): 80–83.

7.   F. Alan Lindberg, *Correlation of Stratigraphic Units of North America (COSUNA)*, Correlation Charts Series (Tulsa, OK: American Association of Petroleum Geologists, 1986).

8.   Andrew A. Snelling, "The Geology of Israel within the Biblical Creation-Flood Framework of History: 2. The Flood Rocks," *Answers Research Journal* 3 (2010): 267–309.

9.   L. L. Sloss, "Sequences in the Cratonic Interior of North America," *Geological Society of America Bulletin* 74 (1963): 93–114.

10.   For a fuller treatment and further information see: John D. Morris, *The Young Earth* (Green Forest, AR: Master Books, 2000), pp. 106–109. Andrew A. Snelling, *Earth's Catastrophic Past: Geology, Creation and the Flood* (Dallas, TX: Institute for Creation Research, 2009), pp. 528–530, 597–605.

11.   Marcus Ross, "Those Not-So-Dry Bones," *Answers*, Jan.–Mar. 2010, pp. 43–45.

12.   A. L. McDonald and R. H. Gunst, "An Analysis of the Earth's Magnetic Field from 1835 to 1965," *ESSA Technical Report*, IER 46-IES 1 (Washington, D.C.: U.S. Government Printing Office, 1967).

13.   R. T. Merrill and M. W. McElhinney, *The Earth's Magnetic Field* (London: Academic Press, 1983), pp. 101–106.

14.   These measurements were gathered by the International Geomagnetic Reference Field. See D. Russell Humphreys, "The Earth's Magnetic Field Is Still Losing Energy," *Creation Research Society Quarterly* 39, no. 1 (2002): 1–11.

15.   Thomas G. Barnes, "Decay of the Earth's Magnetic Field and the Geochronological Implications," *Creation Research Society Quarterly* 8, no. 1 (1971): 24–29; Thomas G. Barnes, *Origin and Destiny of the Earth's Magnetic Field*, Technical Monograph no. 4, 2nd edition (Santee, CA: Institute for Creation Research, 1983).

16.   D. Russell Humphreys, "Reversals of the Earth's Magnetic Field During the Genesis Flood," in *Proceedings of the First International Conference on Creationism*, vol. 2, R. E. Walsh, C. L. Brooks, and R. S. Crowell, eds. (Pittsburgh, PA: Creation Science Fellowship, 1986), pp. 113–126.

17.   For a fuller treatment and further information see: John D. Morris, *The Young Earth* (Green Forest, AR: Master Books, 2000), pp. 74–85. Andrew A. Snelling, *Earth's Catastrophic Past: Geology, Creation and the Flood* (Dallas, TX: Institute for Creation Research, 2009), pp. 873–877.

18.   L. J. Lanzerotti, et al., "Measurements of the Large-Scale Direct-Current Earth Potential and Possible Implications for the Geomagnetic Dynamo," *Science* 229, no. 4708 (1985): 47–49.

19.   D. Russell Humphreys, "Can Evolutionists Now Explain the Earth's Magnetic Field?" *Creation Research Society Quarterly* 33, no. 3 (1996): 184–185;

20.   D. Russell Humphreys, "Physical Mechanism for Reversal of the Earth's Magnetic Field During the Flood," in *Proceedings of the Second International Conference on Creationism*, vol. 2, R. E. Walsh and C. L. Brooks, eds. (Pittsburgh, PA: Creation Science Fellowship, 1990), pp. 129–142.

21.   R. V. Gentry, G. L. Glish, and E. H. McBay, "Differential Helium Retention in Zircons: Implications for Nuclear Waste Containment," *Geophysical Research Letters* 9, no. 10 (1982): 1129–1130.

22. S. W. Reiners, K. A. Farley, and H. J. Hicks, "He Diffusion and (U-Th)/He Thermochronometry of Zircon: Initial Results from Fish Canyon Tuff and Gold Butte, Nevada," *Tectonophysics* 349, no. 1–4 (2002): 297–308. D. Russell Humphreys, et al., "Helium Diffusion Rates Support Accelerated Nuclear Decay," in *Proceedings of the Fifth International Conference on Creationism*, R. L. Ivey, Jr. (Pittsburgh, PA: Creation Science Fellowship, 2003), ed., pp. 175–196. D. Russell Humphreys, "Young Helium Diffusion Age of Zircons Supports Accelerated Nuclear Decay," in *Radioisotopes and the Age of the Earth: Results of a Young-Earth Creationist Research Initiative*, L. Vardiman, A.A. Snelling and E. F. Chaffin, eds. (El Cajon, CA: Institute for Creation Research, and Chino Valley, AZ: Creation Research Society, 2005), pp. 25–100.

23. Humphreys et al., 2003; Humphreys, 2005.

24. Andrew A. Snelling, "Radiometric dating: Back to Basics," *Answers* 4, no. 3 (July–Sept. 2009): 72–75; Andrew A. Snelling, "Radiometric Dating: Problems With the Assumptions," *Answers* 4, no. 4 (Oct.–Dec. 2009): 70–73.

25. G. E. Hutchinson, "Marginalia," *American Scientist* 35 (1947): 118; Melvin A. Cook, "Where Is the Earth's Radiogenic Helium?" Nature 179, no. 4557 (1957): 213.

26. J. C. G. Walker, *Evolution of the Atmosphere* (London: Macmillan, 1977); J. W. Chamberlain and D.M. Hunten, Theory of Planetary Atmospheres, 2nd edition (London: Academic Press, 1987).

27. Larry Vardiman, *The Age of the Earth's Atmosphere: A Study of the Helium Flux Through the Atmosphere* (El Cajon, CA: Institute for Creation Research, 1990).

28. For a fully treatment and further information see: John D. Morris, *The Young Earth* (Green Forest, AR: Master Books, 2000), pp. 83–85. Don B. DeYoung, *Thousands . . . Not Billions* (Green Forest, AR: Master Books, 2005), pp. 65–78. Andrew A. Snelling, *Earth's Catastrophic Past: Geology, Creation and the Flood* (Dallas, TX: Institute for Creation Research, 2009), pp. 887–890.

29. D. Russell Humphreys, et al., "Helium Diffusion Age of 6,000 Years Supports Accelerated Nuclear Decay," *Creation Research Society Quarterly* 41, no. 1 (2004): 1–16.

30. Humphreys, 2005.

31. D. Russell Humphreys, "Critics of Helium Evidence for a Young World Now Seem Silent," *Journal of Creation* 24, no. 1 (2010): 14–16. D. Russell Humphreys, "Critics of Helium Evidence for a Young World Now Seem Silent?" *Journal of Creation* 24, no. 3 (2010): 35–39.

32. Robert L. Whitelaw, "Time, Life, and History in the Light of 15,000 Radiocarbon Dates," *Creation Research Society Quarterly* 7, no. 1 (1970): 56–71.

33. Paul Giem, "Carbon-14 Content of Fossil Carbon," *Origins* 51 (2001): 6–30.

34. John R. Baumgardner, et al., "Measurable 14C in Fossilized Organic Materials: Confirming the Young Earth Creation-Flood Model," in *Proceedings of the Fifth International Conference on Creationism*, R. L. Ivey, Jr., ed. (Pittsburgh, PA: Creation Science Fellowship, 2003), pp. 127–142.

35. John R. Baumgardner, "14C Evidence for a Recent Global Flood and a Young Earth," in Radioisotopes and the *Age of the Earth: Results of a Young-Earth Creationist Research Initiative*, L. Vardiman, A. A. Snelling, and E. F. Chaffin, eds. (El Cajon, CA: Institute for Creation Research, and Chino Valley, AZ: Creation Research Society, 2005), pp. 587–630.

36. For a fuller treatment and further information see: Don B. DeYoung, *Thousands . . . Not Billions* (Green Forest, AR: Master Books, 2005), pp. 45–62. Andrew A. Snelling, *Earth's Catastrophic Past: Geology, Creation and the Flood* (Dallas, TX: Institute for Creation Research, 2009), pp. 855–864. Andrew A. Snelling, "Carbon-14 Dating—Understanding the Basics," *Answers* 5, no. 4 (Oct.–Dec. 2010): 72–75. Andrew A. Snelling, "Carbon-14 in Fossils and Diamonds—an Evolution Dilemma" *Answers* 6, no. 1 (Jan.–Mar. 2011): 72–75. Andrew A. Snelling, "50,000-Year-Old Fossils—A Creationist Puzzle," *Answers* 6, no. 2 (April–June 2011): 70–73.

37. Andrew A. Snelling, "Radiocarbon Ages for Fossil Ammonites and Wood in Cretaceous

Strata near Redding, California," *Answers Research Journal* 1 (2008): 123–144.

38. Baumgardner, 2005, pp. 614–616.

39. M. Meybeck, "Concentrations des eaux fluvials en majeurs et apports en solution aux oceans," *Revue de Géologie Dynamique et de Géographie Physique* 21, no. 3 (1979): 215.

40. F. L. Sayles and P. C. Mangelsdorf, "Cation-Exchange Characteristics of Amazon with Suspended Sediment and Its Reaction with Seawater," *Geochimica et Cosmochimica Acta* 43 (1979): 767–779.

41. Steven A. Austin and D. Russell Humphreys, "The Sea's Missing Salt: A Dilemma for Evolutionists," in *Proceedings of the Second International Conference on Creationism*, R. E. Walsh and C. L. Brooks, eds., volume 2 (Pittsburgh, PA: Creation Science Fellowship, 1990), pp. 17–33.

42. For a fuller treatment and further information see: John D. Morris, The Young Earth (Green Forest, AR: Master Books, 2000), pp. 85–87. Andrew A. Snelling, *Earth's Catastrophic Past: Geology, Creation and the Flood* (Dallas, TX: Institute for Creation Research, 2009), pp. 879–881.

43. Austin and Humphreys, 1990.

44. Glenn R. Morton, pers. comm., *Salt in the sea*, http://www.asa3.org/archive/evolution/199606/0051.html.

45. Calculations based on many other seawater elements give much younger ages for the ocean, too. See Stuart A. Nevins (Steven A. Austin), "Evolution: The Oceans Say No!" *Impact* no. 8. (Santee, CA: Institute for Creation Research, 1973).

Dr. Andrew Snelling is director of research at Answers in Genesis. He holds a PhD in geology from the University of Sydney and has worked as a consultant research geologist in both Australia and America. He is the author of numerous scientific articles.

Dr. David Menton holds a PhD in cell biology from Brown University and is a well-respected author and teacher. He is Professor Emeritus at the Washington University School of Medicine in St. Louis. Dr. Menton has many published works and is a speaker and researcher for Answers in Genesis.

Dr. Danny Faulkner is a speaker, researcher, and astronomer for Answers in Genesis. He holds a PhD in astronomy from Indiana University and was a full professor at The University of South Carolina Lancaster. He has written numerous articles in astronomical journals, and is the author of *Universe by Design*.

Dr. Georgia Purdom is a speaker and researcher for Answers in Genesis. She earned her doctorate from Ohio State University in molecular genetics and spent six years as a professor of biology at Mt. Vernon Nazarene University.

The Hubble telescope as seen after its last servicing in 2009.
Photo courtesy of NASA.

Does Astronomy Confirm a Young Universe?

by Don B. DeYoung and Jason Lisle

One of the common objections to biblical creation is that scientists have supposedly demonstrated that the universe is much older than the Bible teaches. The first chapter of Genesis clearly teaches that God created all things in six days ("ordinary" days as defined by an evening and morning) and that human beings were created on the sixth day. This is confirmed and clarified in the other Scriptures as well (e.g., Exodus 20:8–11; Mark 10:6). And since the Bible records about four thousand years between Adam and Christ (Genesis 5:3–32), the biblical age of the universe is about 6,000 years. This stands in stark contrast with the generally accepted secular age estimate of 4.6 billion years for the earth, and three times longer still, 13.7 billion years, for the universe beyond.

This fundamental time discrepancy is no small matter. It is obvious that if the secular age estimate is correct, then the Bible is in error and cannot be trusted. Conversely, if the Bible really is what it claims to be, the authoritative Word of God (2 Timothy 3:16), then something is seriously wrong with the secular estimates for the age of the universe. Since the secular time scale challenges the authority of Scripture, Christians must be ready to give an answer—a defense of the biblical time scale (1 Peter 3:15).

The assumptions of age estimates

Why such a difference? What is really going on here? It turns out that all secular age estimates are based on two fundamental (and questionable) assumptions. These are *naturalism* (the belief that nature is all there is),[1] and *uniformitarianism* (the belief that present rates and conditions are generally representative of past rates and conditions).

In order to estimate the age of something (whose age is not known historically), we must have information about how the thing came to be, and how it has changed over time. Secular scientists assume that the earth and universe were not created supernaturally (the assumption of naturalism), and that they generally change in the slow-and-gradual way that we see today (the assumption of uniformitarianism).[2] If these starting assumptions are not correct, then there is no reason to trust the resulting age estimates.

But notice something about the assumptions of naturalism and uniformitarianism: they are anti-biblical assumptions. The Bible indicates that the universe was created supernaturally by God (Genesis 1:1) and that present rates are not always indicative of past rates (such as the global Flood described in Genesis 7–8). So, by assuming naturalism and uniformitarianism, the secular scientist has already assumed that the Bible is wrong. He then estimates that the universe is very, very old, and concludes that the Bible must be wrong. But this is what he assumed at the start. His argument is circular. It's the logical fallacy called "begging the question." But all old-earth (and old-universe) arguments assume naturalism and uniformitarianism. Therefore, they are all fallacious circular arguments. That's right—all of them.

Refuting an old earth and universe

A much better way to argue for the age of the universe is to hypothetically assume the opposite of what you are trying to prove, and then show that such an assumption leads to inconsistencies. In other words, we temporarily assume naturalism and uniformitarianism for the sake of argument, and then show that even when we use those assumptions, the universe appears to be much younger than secular scientists claim. This technique is called a *reductio ad absurdum* (reduction to absurdity). So the secular worldview is unreasonable since it is inconsistent with itself. In the following arguments, we will temporarily assume (for the sake of argument) that naturalism and uniformitarianism are true, and then show that the evidence still indicates a solar system much younger than the secular estimate of 4.6 billion years, and a universe much younger than 13.7 billion years.

Moon recession

Our nearest neighbor, the moon, has much to contribute to the recent creation worldview. A parade of lunar origin theories has passed by over the decades. These include fission of the moon from the earth (1960s), capture of the moon by earth's gravity from elsewhere in space (1970s), and formation of the moon from the collapse of a dust cloud or nebula (1980s). The currently popular model calls for lunar origin by an ancient collision of the earth with a Mars-size space object. All such natural origin theories are unconvincing and temporary; a recent supernatural creation remains the only credible explanation. Inquiry into origins need not be limited to natural science alone, as often assumed. The historical definition of science is the search for truth. If God is indeed the Creator, then scientists should not arbitrarily dismiss this fact. Many feel that modern science has been impoverished by its artificial limitation to naturalism, or secularism.

The moon reveals multiple design features. Lunar tides keep our oceans healthy, protecting marine life. The moon's (roughly circular) orbit stabilizes the earth's tilt and seasons. The moon also provides us with a night light, compass, clock, and calendar. The extent to which the moon controls the biorhythms of plants and animals, both on land and in the sea, is not well understood but is surely essential to life.

The moon also instructs us concerning the age of the earth. Consider the gravitational tide force between the earth and moon. This interaction also results in a very gradually receding moon, and slowing of the earth's rotation. These changes are highly dependent on the earth-moon separation, and are in direct conflict with the evolutionary time scale. Figure 1 shows the spinning earth and orbiting moon. A slight delay in the earth's high tides (the dark bumps) results in a forward pull on the moon, causing it to slowly spiral outward from the earth. In turn, the moon's gravity pulls back on the earth, slightly decreasing its spin.

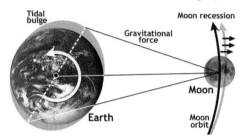

Figure 1: The moon is slowly drifting away from the earth, but the rate of recession would have been much faster in the past.

Currently, the moon is moving outward from the earth by 3.82 cm/yr (1.5 in/yr). However, this recession is highly nonlinear and would have been greater in the past. If one assumes unlimited extrapolation back in time, gravity theory shows the moon in direct physical contact with earth about 1.55 billion years ago.[3] This is not to say that the moon was ever this near or this old. In fact, a moon located anywhere in the vicinity of the earth would be fragmented, resulting in a Saturn-like ring of debris encircling the earth. This follows because the earth's gravity force would overcome the moon's own cohesive force. The tides lead to a limited time scale for the moon, far less than 1.55 billion years. However, evolutionists assume that the moon and solar system are 4.6 billion years old. Also, life is said to have originated on earth about 3.5 billion years ago. The fundamental problem with the evolutionary time scale is obvious.

On a much shorter time scale, 6,000 years, the moon has moved outward by only about 755 feet (230 m) since its creation. Therefore, the creationist suggestion is that the moon was placed in orbit close to its present earth distance. Due to the earth's rotational slowing, the length of a day 6,000 years ago is calculated to be just 0.12 seconds shorter than at present.

Comets

Comets silently orbit the sun and put on occasional majestic displays in our night sky. Each year, dozens of comets loop the sun. About one-half of them have been named and studied on previous orbits. These comets don't last forever. Sooner or later they may be ejected from the solar system, may collide with the sun or planets, or they may break into fragments like a poorly packed snowball. There are clouds of dusty debris in the solar system, ghosts of disintegrated comets from the past. When the earth happens to pass through such a cloud, it sweeps up some of this comet dust. Then we see "shooting stars," an echo of the comet's original light show. In a spectacular 1994 display, comet Shoemaker-Levi was destroyed when it collided with Jupiter. The gravity of the massive outer planets protects the earth from similar comet collisions.

The question arises, why do comets still exist in the solar system? On a time scale of multiple billions of years, should they not all be long gone, either by escape, collision, or disintegration? The average number of solar revolutions before a comet dissipates is estimated to be about 40 trips. Comet Halley has already been observed through at least 28 orbits, dating back to 240 B.C. Its remaining years are numbered.

Astronomers recognize two comet varieties with respectively short and long revolving periods. The short-period comets have orbit times less than about 200 years. Halley's Comet is such an example with a period of about 76 years. Meanwhile, the long-period comets may require thousands of years for each solar pass. The origin of both kinds of comets remains a mystery to secular astronomers. Based on the rate at which comets are destroyed today, it is surprising (from an old-universe perspective) that either long-period or shortperiod comets are still present. The supply should have been depleted billions of years ago. How then do secular astronomers explain these apparently "young" comets in a solar system that they believe to be billions of years old?

To account for this paradox, secular astronomers have proposed that myriads of icy, comet-sized objects formed early in the solar system and continue to orbit at a tremendous distance from the sun where they remain permanently frozen for billions of years. It is suggested that every now and then one of these objects is dislodged from its distant orbit and injected into the inner solar systemto become a new comet. According to this idea, as old comets are destroyed,new ones replace them.

Two present-day comet reservoirs are suggested by astronomers: one to supply short-period comets, the other to account for long-period comets. The Kuiper belt is thought to exist on the outer fringe of the known solar system, named for astronomer Gerald Kuiper (1905–1973). More than one hundred large, icy objects have been observed beyond planet Neptune, and multitudes more are assumed. It is thought that these trans-Neptunian objects (TNOs) are the largest members of the Kuiper belt. It is assumed that the unseen smaller members of the Kuiper belt occasionally fall inward toward the sun to become short-period comets. Hundreds of times further outward from Neptune is an assumed, vast Oort cloud of icy masses, named for Jan Oort (1900–1992). It is further assumed that a passing star may disturb this remote cloud from time to time, deflecting some of these icy objects toward the inner solar system, thereby replenishing the supply of long-period comets.

So far, the only objects detected at these great distances are much larger than any known comet. The existence of vast Kuiper and Oort clouds of actual cometsized objects is not verifiable with current technology. The simplest explanation would appear to line up with the biblical time scale: the presence of comets may be evidence that the solar system is not nearly as old as is often assumed. Comets teach us two valuable lessons. First, their eventual loss is a reminder of the temporary nature of the solar system and universe. As Psalm 102:25–26 describes it:

> . . . the heavens are the work of Your hands. They will perish, but You will endure; Yes, they will all grow old like a garment.

As a second lesson, the exact motions of comets, planets, and stars are elegant evidence of God's controlling presence throughout the physical universe.

Faint young sun paradox

Astronomers use the term stellar evolution for the aging process of stars. Our sun is assumed to be in its midlife stage, 4.6 billion years of age, as it gradually converts its hydrogen to helium via nuclear fusion reactions in its core. However, a basic time problem arises. Computer modeling of the sun on an evolutionary time scale predicts that the sun must gradually brighten. If true, the sun would be 30 percent dimmer during the period 3.8–2.5 billion years ago. The early earth would have been locked in a global ice age, with the crust and seas frozen solid. This in turn precludes the development of early life on earth.

In conflict with the icy prediction of solar models, geologic evidence points to an earth that was warmer in the past (irrespective of the time scale). This means that there is a fundamental problem with the unlimited extrapolation back in time of solar energy output. The creationist alternative is that the sun was placed in the heavens, on Day 4 of the creation week, with a temperature very close to that of the present day.

Rapid star aging

Stellar evolution might better be called star decay or degeneration. Current models predict very gradual changes in the nature of stars. The sun, for example, is predicted to pass through several stages in coming ages. At present it is called a "main sequence" star. In the distant future, it is predicted to expand in size and grow cooler as it becomes a red giant star. Following this, the sun reverts to a small, hot white dwarf star. Each stage is assumed to last for millions of years.

Observations suggest that some stars may age much more rapidly than generally believed. For example, consider Sirius, the brightest nighttime star. At a distance of 8.6 light years from earth, it is known as the Dog Star, prominent in the Canis Major constellation. Sirius has a dwarf companion star, and there is intriguing evidence that this dwarf may have formed from a red giant in just the past 1,000 years. Historical records, including those of Ptolemy, describe Sirius as red or pink in color. The suggestion is that the red giant companion dominated the pair at this early time. Today, Sirius is a brilliant blue-white color and its dwarf companion is basically invisible. Other stars also occasionally show unexpected color changes, indicating possible rapid aging processes. Such events call into question the fundamental time scale of current stellar evolution models.

Spiral galaxies

Spiral galaxies also pose a problem for the secular time scale. Spiral galaxies contain blue stars in their arms. But blue stars are very luminous and expend their fuel quickly. They cannot last billions of years. Secular astronomers realize this and so they simply assume that new blue stars form continuously (from collapsing clouds of gas) to replenish the supply. However, star formation is riddled with theoretical problems. It has never been observed, nor could it truly be observed since the process is supposed to take hundreds of thousands of years. Gas in space is very resistant to being compressed into a star. Compression of gas causes an increase in magnetic field strength, gas pressure, and angular momentum, which would all tend to prevent any further compression into a star. Although these problems may not be insurmountable, we should be very skeptical of star formation—especially given the lack of observational support.

Perhaps even more compelling is the fact that spiral arms cannot last billions of years. The spiral arms of galaxies rotate differentially—meaning the inner portions rotate faster than the outer portions. Every spiral galaxy is essentially twisting itself up—becoming tighter and tighter with time. In far less than one billion years, the galaxy should be twisted to the point where the arms are no longer recognizable. Many galaxies are supposed to be ten billion years old in the secular view, yet their spiral arms are easily recognizable. The spiral structure of galaxies strongly suggests that they are much younger than generally accepted.

There is a common misunderstanding here because people sometimes confuse linear velocity with angular velocity. Many people have heard or read that spiral galaxies have a nearly "flat" rotation curve—meaning that stars near the edge have about the same linear speed as stars near the core. This is true—but it doesn't alleviate the problem. In fact it is the cause. A star near the core makes a very small circle when it orbits, whereas a star near the edge makes a very large circle—which takes much longer if the star travels at the same speed. So in physics terminology we say that the stars have the same speed, but the inner star has a greater angular velocity because it completes an orbit in far less time than the outer star. This is why spiral galaxies rotate differentially.

Additionally, some people are under the mistaken impression that dark matter was hypothesized to alleviate the spiral wind-up problem. But this is not so. Dark matter explains (possibly) why the stars have a flat rotation curve to begin with. It does not explain how a spiral structure could last billions of years.

To get around the spiral galaxy wind-up problem, secular astronomers have proposed the "spiral density wave hypothesis." In this model, as the spiral arms become twisted and homogenized, new spiral arms are formed to replace the old ones. The new arms are supposed to form by a pressure wave that travels around the galaxy, triggering star formation. If this idea were true, then galaxies could be ten billion years old, whereas their arms are constantly being merged and reformed.

However, the spiral density wave hypothesis may create more problems than it solves. There are difficulties in creating such a pressure wave in the first place. The spiral density wave hypothesis cannot easily explain why galactic magnetic fields are aligned with the spiral arms (since magnetic fields move with the material—not with pressure waves); nor can it easily account for the tight spiral structure near the core of some galaxies such as M51. Perhaps most significantly, the spiral density wave hypothesis presupposes that star formation is possible. We have already seen that this is a dubious assumption at best. The simplest, most straightforward explanation for spiral galaxies is the biblical one: God created them thousands of years ago.

Conclusion

Many more such evidences for a young earth, solar system, and universe could be listed. Space does not permit us to discuss in detail how planetary magnetic fields decay far too quickly to last billions of years, or how the internal heat of the giant planets suggests they are not as old as is claimed. In all cases, the age estimates are far too young to be compatible with an old universe. It should be noted that all these age estimates are an upper limit—they denote the maximum possible, not the actual age. So they are all compatible with the biblical time scale, but challenge the notion of an old universe.

It should also be noted that in all cases we have (for argument's sake) based the estimate on the assumptions of our critics. That is, we have assumed hypothetically that both naturalism and uniformitarianism are true, and yet we still find that the estimated ages come out far younger than the old-universe view requires. This shows that the old-universe view is internally inconsistent. It does not comport with its own assumptions. However, the biblical view is self-consistent. As with other fields of science, the evidence from astronomy confirms that the Bible is true. The answer to the title of this chapter is a resounding yes—the heavens declare a recent, supernatural creation!

References and resources for further study

Don B. DeYoung, *Astronomy and Creation* (Winona Lake, IN: BMH Books, 2010).

Danny Faulkner, *Universe by Design* (Green Forest, AR: Master Books, 2004).

Jason Lisle, *Taking Back Astronomy* (Green Forest, AR: Master Books, 2006).

Jason Lisle, *The Ultimate Proof of Creation* (Green Forest, AR: Master Books, 2009).

1. Some scientists hold to a softer form of naturalism called "methodological naturalism." This is the concept that a supernatural realm may indeed exist, but should not be considered when doing scientific study. For all intents and purposes, the naturalist does not accept that there is anything beyond nature—at least when he or she is doing science.

2. Uniformitarianism is a matter of degree. Some secular scientists are willing to accept that catastrophes play a major role in the shaping of the earth's features. However, virtually all of them deny the worldwide Flood, which would have been the most significant geological event in earth's history since its creation. In this sense, virtually all secular scientists embrace uniformitarianism to a large extent.

3. Don B. DeYoung, "Tides and the Creation Worldview," *Creation Research Society Quarterly*, 45 no. 2 (2008): 100–108.

Dr. Don B. DeYoung is chairman of physical science at Grace College, Indiana. He holds a BS in physics from Michigan Technological University, an MS in physics from Michigan Technical University, and a PhD in physics from Iowa State University. He has published technical papers in the *Journal of Chemical Physics* and the *Creation Research Society Quarterly*. Dr. DeYoung is the author of eight books on Bible-science topics.

Dr. Jason Lisle holds a PhD in astrophysics from the University of Colorado at Boulder. Dr. Lisle is a popular author and speaker on the topics of creation and apologetics. He is currently the Director of Research at the Institute for Creation Research.

How Old Does the Earth Look?

by Andrew Snelling

*I*nsisting that the earth and the universe are young, only 6,000 years old or so, does not make the biblical view popular in today's enlightened "scientific" culture. It would be so easy just to go along with the view believed and followed by the overwhelming majority of scientists—and taught in nearly all universities and museums around the world—that the universe is 13–14 billion years old and the earth 4.5 billion years old.

After all, many Christians and most scientists who are Christians believe in such a vast antiquity for the earth and universe. Consequently, they even insist the days in Genesis 1 were not literal days, but were countless millions of years long. Also, they claim the Genesis account of creation by God is just poetic and/or figurative, so it is not meant to be read as history.

Why a young age for the earth?

Of course, the reason for insisting on a young earth and universe is because other biblical authors took Genesis as literal history and an eyewitness account provided and guaranteed accurate by the Creator Himself (2 Timothy 3:16a; 2 Peter 1:21). Jesus also took Genesis as literal history (Mark 10:6–9; Matthew 19:4–5; Luke 17:27). So, the outcome of letting Scripture interpret Scripture is a young earth and universe.

The Hebrew language and context used in Genesis 1 can only mean literal (24 hour) days.[1] Furthermore, as history, the genealogies in Genesis 5 and 11 provide an accurate chronology, so that from the creation of the first man Adam to the present day is only about 6,000 years. Since the earth was only created five literal days before Adam, then on the authority of God's Word the earth is only about 6,000 years old.

Does the earth look old?

Nevertheless, most people, including Christians, would still claim dogmatically that the earth looks old. But why does the earth supposedly look old? And how old does the earth really look? If we rightly ask such questions, then we are likely to get closer to the right answers.

The use of the word looks gives us the necessary clue to finding the answers. Looking at an object and making a judgment about it requires two operations by the observer. There is first the observation of the object with one's eyes. Light impulses then go from the eyes to be processed by one's brain. How one's brain interprets what has been seen through one's eyes is dependent on what information is already stored in one's brain. Such information has been progressively acquired and stored in our brains since birth. So, for example, as a child we learn what a rock is by being shown a rock.

Trilobite fossils in sandstone

We observe that a sandstone is made of sand cemented together, and we see a trilobite fossil inside the sandstone, so we wonder how the trilobite came to be fossilized in the sandstone and how both the sandstone and the trilobite fossil formed. However, we never actually observed either the trilobite being buried by sand and fossilized or the deposition of the sand and its cementation into sandstone. Therefore, we don't really know how and when the trilobite fossil and the sandstone formed—so just by looking at them we really don't know how old they are.

How, then, can we work out how old they might be and how they formed? Because we can't go back to the past, it seems logical to think in terms of what we see happening around us today—in the present. Today rivers slowly erode land surfaces and gradually transport the sand downstream to their mouths where they build deltas. The sediments also are eventually spread gradually out on the sea floor, where bottom-dwelling creatures like trilobites could perhaps be occasionally buried and then fossilized.

So, with this apparently logical scenario in our minds, based on our everyday experience, when we look at that piece of sandstone with the trilobite fossil in it, it seems totally reasonable to conclude that, because it took such a long time to erode and transport the sand and then deposit it to bury and fossilize the trilobite, the sandstone and trilobite fossil must be very old. Perhaps they may even be millions of years old. However, it needs to be remembered that there are no particular intrinsic features of the sandstone and the trilobite fossil that are incontestably diagnostic of any supposed great age. The conclusion that they must be old wasn't because they actually look old, but because it was assumed they took a long time to form based on present-day experience.

Long age reasoning questioned

Now let's extend this reasoning to the earth itself. Why is it that most people think the earth looks old? Isn't it because they assume it took a long time to form based on their present-day experience of geological processes? After all, volcanic eruptions only occur sporadically today, so the vast, thick lava flows stacked on top of one another—for example, in the USA's Pacific Northwest—must have taken a long time to accumulate. However, this reasoning is wrong for three very valid reasons.

First, it ignores the fact that we cannot go back to the past to actually verify by direct observations that vast, thick stacks of lava flows—and sandstones with trilobite fossils—took a long time to form millions of years ago. The inference that the present is the key to the past is only an assumption, not a fact.

Second, that assumption deliberately ignores the fact that we do have direct eyewitnesses from the past who have told us what did happen to the earth and how old it really is. The Bible claims to be the communication to us of the Creator God who has always existed. Its authenticity is overwhelmingly verified by countless exactly fulfilled predictions, archeological and scientific evidences, corroborating eyewitness accounts, and the changed lives and testimonies of Bible-believing Christians. In Genesis 1–11, it is revealed how to calculate the age of the earth, and how rock layers and fossils were rapidly and recently formed in the year-long, global, catastrophic Flood.

And third, there is now abundant scientific evidence that rock layers and fossils can only form rapidly due to catastrophic geological processes not usually seen today, and not on the scale they must have occurred at in the past.[2]

Catastrophism today

Geologists are always studying present-day geological processes, including rare catastrophic events, such as floods, earthquakes, and violent volcanic eruptions. Such processes have been observed to produce and change geological features very rapidly;

so, geologists have learned not to ignore such currently rare catastrophic events when interpreting how the earth's features were produced in the past.

Further examples of why most people think the earth looks old are river valleys and canyons. Because the rivers in most valleys and canyons today seem to only slowly and imperceptibly erode their channels, even during occasional floods, most people assume it must have taken millions of years to erode valleys and canyons.

This canyon system, with 100-feet high cliffs, was eroded adjacent to Mount St. Helens in less than a day! Photo courtesy Institute for Creation Research.

However, the observational realities are more instructive than such an erroneous assumption. For example, since the Colorado River today does not erode its channel, the only truly viable explanation for the carving of the Grand Canyon is rapid catastrophic erosion on an enormous scale by dammed waters left over from the global Genesis Flood.[3] Such rapid catastrophic erosion carving canyons has even been observed. As a result of the 1980 and subsequent eruptions at Mount St. Helens, up to 600 feet of rock layers rapidly accumulated nearby. A mudflow on March 18, 1982, eroded a canyon system over 100 feet deep in these sediment layers, resulting in a one-fortieth scale model of the real Grand Canyon.[4]

Uniformitarianism predicted

In 2 Peter 3, we read a prediction that Peter made around AD 62 that scoffers would arise who would challenge and deny that God created the earth and subsequently destroyed the earth by the cataclysmic global Flood. Peter says they would be willingly ignorant and deliberately reject the evidence for a created earth and the year-long global Flood. They would claim instead that the present is the key to the past, that present-day geological processes have always operated at today's snail's pace and that they alone are necessary to explain how rock layers and fossils formed and how old the earth is.

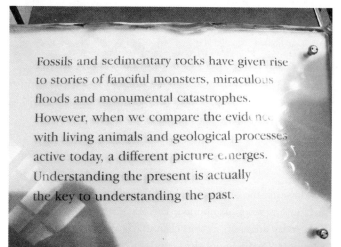

Fossils and sedimentary rocks have given rise to stories of fanciful monsters, miraculous floods and monumental catastrophes. However, when we compare the evidence with living animals and geological processes active today, a different picture emerges. Understanding the present is actually the key to understanding the past.

Secular museum display teaching the uniformitarian concept that understanding the present is the key to understanding the past

This prediction was actually fulfilled about 200 years ago—about 1750 years after the prediction was made. James Hutton, a doctor and farmer-turned-geologist, claimed in his 1785 Royal Society of Edinburgh paper and 1795 book *Theory of the Earth* that he saw "no vestige of a beginning" for the earth because present-day geological processes have slowly recycled rock materials over vast eons of time. This was a deliberate rejection of the biblical account of the recent, global catastrophic Flood, up until that time accepted by most scholars to be the explanation for fossil-bearing rock layers. Indeed, Hutton insisted that "the past history of our globe must be explained by what can be seen happening now" (emphasis mine).[5]

It was Charles Lyell, a lawyer-turned-geologist, with his three volume 1830–33 Principles of Geology who eventually convinced the geological establishment to abandon the biblical Flood in favor of this "principle" he called uniformitarianism. Lyell openly declared that he wanted to remove the influence of Moses (the human author of Genesis) from geology, revealing his motivation was spiritual, not scientific.[6] He insisted on the uniformity through time of natural processes only at today's rates, a belief that was later encapsulated in the phrase "the present is the key to the past."

This is the belief that now underpins virtually all modern geological explanations about the earth and its rock layers. And it is a belief, because it cannot be proved that only today's geological processes can explain the earth's history and determine its age. No one has ever observed past geological processes, except for God—and Noah and his family—during the Flood when these processes were definitely catastrophic on a global scale. Yet most people today, even Christians, have unwittingly imbibed this uniformitarian belief, having been brainwashed by the constant barrage of teaching globally over many decades by the world's education systems (schools, colleges, and universities), museums and media (newspapers, magazines, television, and even Hollywood). Indeed, most people automatically see the earth as old because they have accepted it is a proven scientific fact that it is old!

Using the right glasses

However, based on the authority of God's Word, we can dogmatically say they are absolutely wrong. Looking at the world through "glasses" that are based on human reasoning alone (man's word) makes people wrongly think the earth looks really old. On the other hand, when we as Christians see the world through the biblical "glasses" provided by God's inerrant Word—so that we see the world as God sees it—we can assert unashamedly that the earth does not really look that old at all, being only about 6,000 years old (which, of course, is young). Indeed, the earth we see today is the way it looks because it is the destroyed remains of the original earth God created, still marred by the subsequent Curse. Furthermore, not only should we understand that the Bible provides the true history of the earth, but that history tells us the earth only looks the way it does today because of what happened in the past. In other words, the past is the key to the present!

Conclusion

In 2 Corinthians 11:3, Paul warns us about the way Satan subtly beguiled the mind of Eve in the Garden of Eden by questioning and twisting God's Word. Today, Satan has subtly beguiled so many people, including Christians, by twisting the clear testimony of God's Word that "the past is the key to the present" into "the present is the key to the past." And just as he used the appealing look of the fruit on that tree to entice Eve, so he uses the snail's pace of geological processes today to make people doubt or deny what God has told us about the young age of the earth and His eyewitness account of the formation of the rock layers and fossils. It also must be emphasized that even though we must trust God and His Word by faith alone (Hebrews 11:3), it is neither an unreasonable nor a subjective faith. This is because God is not a man that He should lie, so the evidence we see in God's world will always ultimately be consistent with what we read in God's Word. Thus, when we put on our biblical "glasses," we should be able to immediately see and recognize the overwhelming evidence that the earth looks and is young and that the earth's fossil-bearing rock layers are a product of the global catastrophic Flood.

After all, if the Genesis Flood really did occur, what evidence would we look for? Genesis 7 says all the high hills and mountains under the whole heaven were covered by the water from the fountains of the great deep and the global torrential rainfall so that all land-dwelling, air-breathing creatures not on the Ark perished. Wouldn't we, therefore, expect to find the remains of billions of plants and creatures buried in rock layers rapidly laid down by water all around the earth? Yes, of course! And that's exactly what we find—billions of rapidly buried fossils in rock layers up on the continents, rapidly deposited by the ocean waters rising up and over the continents all around the earth. This confirms that the rocks and fossils aren't millions of years old—and neither is the earth.

So how old does the earth look? If we look at the earth through the "glasses" of human reasoning—that only snail-paced present geological processes can explain the past—then the earth does indeed look old. However, that autonomous human reasoning blatantly denies what God's Word clearly tells us about the true age of the God-created earth and about what happened in the recent past during the global cataclysmic Flood, which is the key to understanding why the earth looks the way it does today.

1. S.W. Boyd, "Statistical Determination of Genre in Biblical Hebrew: Evidence for an Historical Reading of Genesis 1:1–2:3, in *Radioisotopes and the Age of the Earth: Results of a Young-Earth Creationist Research Initiative*, eds. L. Vardiman, A.A. Snelling, and E.F. Chaffin (El Cajon, CA: Institute for Creation Research and Chino Valley, AZ: Creation Research Society, 2005), pp. 631–734.

2. S.A. Austin, "Interpreting Strata of Grand Canyon," in *Grand Canyon: Monument to Catastrophe*, ed. S.A. Austin (Santee, CA: Institute for Creation Research, 1994), pp. 21–56; A.A. Snelling, "The World's a Graveyard," *Answers*, April–June, pp. 76–79; J.H. Whitmore, "Aren't Millions of Years Required for Geological Processes?" in *The New Answers Book 2*, ed. K. Ham (Green Forest, AR: Master Books, 2008), pp. 229–244.

3. S.A. Austin, "How was Grand Canyon Eroded?" in *Grand Canyon: Monument to Catastrophe*, ed. S.A. Austin (Santee, CA: Institute for Creation Research, 1994), pp. 83–110.

4. S.A. Austin, "Mount St. Helens and Catastrophism," in *Proceedings of the First International Conference on Creationism*, vol. 1 (Pittsburgh, PA: Creation Science Fellowship, 1986), pp. 3–9.

5. A. Holmes, *Principles of Physical Geology*, 2nd ed., London: Thomas Nelson and Sons, 1965), pp. 43–44, 163.

6. R.S. Porter, "Charles Lyell and the Principles of the History of Geology," *British Journal for the History of Science*, IX, 32, no. 2 (1976): 91–103.

Jacob
ush down our enemies
will trample those

Science or the Bible?

by Ken Ham and Terry Mortenson

Ever heard one of these claims? Perhaps you've even said one your-self. Over the years, we've heard them all—but they're all false, or at least they imply a falsehood.

Common claims by non-Christians:

"Science proves the Bible is wrong."

"Evolution is science, but the Bible is religion."

"Evolutionists believe in science, but creationists reject science."

Common claims by Christians:

"I believe the Bible over science."

"Creation is religion, but evolution is religion, too."

"Creationists believe in the Bible and reject science."

The Bible's account of beginnings cannot be tested in a labora-tory, so secular scientists—and even some Christians—believe it is not science and must be classified as religion.

Secular scientists claim that their view of beginnings (evolu-tion) can be tested in a laboratory, so their view is scientific. For instance, they point to mutated fruit flies or speciation observed in the field (such as new species of mosquitoes or fish).

But this is where many people are confused—what is meant by "science" or "scientific."

Before we get caught up in a debate about whether the Bible or evolution is scientific, we have learned to ask, "Could you please define what you mean by science?" The answer usually reveals where the real problem lies.

Defining science

People are generally unaware that dictionaries give a root meaning, or etymology, of science similar to this one from Webster's: "from Latin *scientia*, from scient-, sciens 'having knowledge,' from present participle of scire 'to know.'"

And most dictionaries give the following meaning of the word: "the state of knowing: knowledge as distinguished from ignorance or misunderstanding."

Although there are other uses of the word, the root meaning of science is basically "knowledge." In fact, in the past, philosophy and theology were considered sciences, and theology was even called the "queen of the sciences."

But over the past 200 years, during the so-called Scientific Revolution, the word science has come to mean a method of knowing, a way of discovering truth. Moreover, many people assume that modern science is the only way to discover truth.

To help people clear up the confusion, we have found it helpful to distinguish between two types of modern science, and compare how each one seeks to discover truth:

1. Operation science uses the so-called "scientific method" to attempt to discover truth, performing observable, repeatable experiments in a controlled environment to find patterns of recurring behavior in the present physical universe. For example, we can test gravity, study the spread of disease, or observe speciation in the lab or in the wild. Both creationists and evolutionists use this kind of science, which has given rise to computers, space shuttles, and cures for diseases.

2. Origin science attempts to discover truth by examining reliable eyewitness testimony (if available); and circumstantial

evidence, such as pottery, fossils, and canyons. Because the past cannot be observed directly, assumptions greatly affect how these scientists interpret what they see.

So, for example, how was the Grand Canyon formed? Was it formed gradually over long periods of time by a little bit of water, or was it formed rapidly by a lot of water? The first interpretation is based on secular assumptions of slow change over millions of years, while the second interpretation is based on biblical assumptions about rapid change during Noah's Flood.

The nature of the debate

At this point, most people realize that the debate is not about operation science, which is based in the present. The debate is about origin science and conflicting assumptions, or beliefs, about the past.

Molecules-to-man evolution is a belief about the past. It assumes, without observing it, that natural processes and lots of time are sufficient to explain the origin and diversification of life.

Of course, evolutionary scientists can test their interpretations using operation science. For instance, evolutionists point to natural selection and speciation—which are observable today. Creation scientists make these same observations, but they recognize that the change has limits and has never been observed to change one kind into another.

Until quite recently, many geologists have used studies of current river erosion and sedimentation to explain how sedimentary rock layers were formed or eroded slowly over millions of years. In the past few decades, however, even secular geologists have begun to recognize that catastrophic processes are a better explanation for many of the earth's rock layers.

Also during this time, creation geologists have been identifying evidence that points to the catastrophic formation of most of the rock record during the unique global Flood of Noah's day.

These present-day observations help us to consider the possible causes of past events, such as the formation of the Grand Canyon. But operation science cannot tell us with certainty what actually happened in the past.

After we explain these two types of science, people usually begin to recognize the potential problems with the statement "evolution is science, but the Bible is religion." Molecules-to-man evolution is not proven by operation science; instead, it is a belief about the past based on antibiblical assumptions.

The Bible, in contrast, is the eyewitness testimony of the Creator, who tells us what happened to produce the earth, the different kinds of life, the fossils, the rock layers, and indeed the whole universe. The Bible gives us the true, "big picture" starting assumptions for origin science.

Different histories

Thus, creationists and evolutionists develop totally different reconstructions of history. But they accept and use the same methods of research in both origin and operation science. The different conclusions about origins arise from different starting assumptions, not the research methods themselves.

So, the battle between the Bible and molecules-to-man evolution is not one of religion versus science. Rather, it is a conflict between worldviews—a creationist's starting assumptions (a biblical worldview) and an evolutionist's starting assumptions (an antibiblical worldview).

The next time someone uses the word science in relation to the creation/evolution controversy, ask him first to define what he means. Only then can you begin to have a fruitful discussion about origins.

Proven facts

Let us be clear. Accurate knowledge (truth) about physical reality can be discovered by the methods of both operation science and origin science. But truth claims in both areas may be false. Many "proven facts" (statements of supposed truth) about how things operate (in physics, chemistry, medicine, etc.), as well as about how things originated (in biology, geology, astronomy, etc.) have been or will be shown to be false. So, as best we can, we must be like the Bereans in Acts 17:11 and examine every truth claim against Scripture and look for faulty logic or false assumptions.

Which worldview is correct?

There are many ways to test the accuracy of the biblical worldview against naturalistic atheism (the worldview that controls most origins research). When our research is based upon biblical truths about the past, we find that our interpretations of the biological and geological facts make sense of what we see in the real world, whereas evolutionary interpretations don't really fit what we see.

Let's look at an example. The Bible says that God created distinct groups of animals "after their kind" (see Genesis 1). Starting with this truth of the Bible as one of our assumptions, we would expect to observe animals divided into distinct groups, or kinds. Creationists postulate that our creative God placed phenomenal variability in the genes of each kind, so there could be considerable variety within each kind. But the preprogrammed mechanism for variation within the kind could never change one kind into a different kind, as evolutionists claim and their belief system requires.

Terry Mortenson earned his doctorate in history of geology from England's University of Coventry and his M.Div. from Trinity Evangelical Divinity School in Deerfield, Illinois. He is a popular writer, speaker, and researcher for Answers in Genesis–USA.

The World: Born in 4004 BC?

by Larry Pierce

The age of the earth is one of the most contentious issues in the creation/evolution debate. In today's culture, the thought of creation occurring about 6,000 years ago is frequently mocked by non-Christians—and also by many Christians.

Archbishop James Ussher (1581–1656) was a highly educated and well-respected historian who devoted his life to defending the Christian faith. Ussher meticulously researched the secular accounts of history and found that the Bible correlated with them. Ussher dedicated several years of his life to compiling a history of the world from creation to AD 70. Today he is greatly ridiculed for declaring that the world was created in 4004 BC.

However, this date was widely accepted until people began to believe in ideas such as billions of years of Earth history. In other words, they started trusting in the latest secular findings based on fallible dating methods, instead of the only absolutely reliable method—consulting the history book provided by the Eyewitness account (the infallible Word of God).

Ussher also argued that Day 1 of creation was October 23. On the surface, this does seem a bit extreme to suggest such a specific date—but when one studies what Ussher did, one quickly realizes he was a brilliant scholar who had very good reasons for his conclusions concerning the date of creation.

Studying Ussher's line of thinking as he arrived at his conclusion—creation on October 23, 4004 BC—provides food for thought to this very day.

The Bible—the basis for Ussher's work

One of Ussher's many projects was to write a complete history of the world in Latin, covering every major event from the time of creation to AD 70. He published this 1,600-page volume in 1650. An English translation entitled *The Annals of the World* was first published in 1658, two years after his death. (The complete work is fascinating. It has recently been translated into modern English and republished.[1])

In preparing this work, Ussher first made the assumption that the Bible is the only reliable source of chronological information for the time periods covered therein. In fact, before the Persian Empire (approximately the sixth to third centuries BC) very little is known from any source about Greek, Roman and Egyptian history or the history of other nations; much rests on speculation and myths. Dates in secular history become more certain with the founding of the Medo-Persian Empire.

For events before this time, Ussher relied solely on data from the Bible to erect his historical framework. He chose the death of King Nebuchadnezzar as a reliable date upon which to anchor all the earlier biblical dates. Working meticulously backward from there, he ended up with his date for creation of October 23, 4004 BC.

How Ussher arrived at the year of creation

Now you ask: How did he get 4004 BC?

Answer: He used the chronologies in the Hebrew text of Genesis 5 and 11, together with other Bible passages that we will consider. To simplify the calculations, Ussher ties the chronology to the final deportation of Judah in 584 BC. His detailed calculations cover over 100 pages in the original document.

How Ussher arrived at Day 1 of creation

Nowhere in your Bible does it say that the day of creation was October 23. Because the Jews and many other ancient peoples started their year in the autumn, Ussher assumed there must be a good reason for it. He therefore concluded that God created the world in the autumn. After consulting astronomical tables, he picked the first Sunday on or after the autumnal equinox to begin the year 4004 BC.

But the equinox occurs around September 21, not October 23. At least, it does now, thanks to some juggling of the calendar. In his research Ussher found that the ancient Jews and the Egyptians did not use the orbit of the moon (lunar calendar) as the basis for their year. Instead, their year was made up of twelve months, each thirty days long. At the end of their year they tacked on five days, and every fourth year they added six days. However, a year of 365 days is too short, and one of exactly 365.25 days is too long. They had to drop days from it every now and then to keep the seasons from drifting.

When Julius Caesar reformed the calendar, he adopted basically the same system we now use, with twelve months of various lengths. However, even with his reforms, the seasons began to drift. By the 1700s the English calendar was off by eleven days. On September 2, 1752, eleven days were dropped from the English calendar to make the seasons start when they were supposed to. Another day was dropped in 1800 and again in 1900. These years would normally have been leap years, but instead were made normal years to keep the calendar in line. Today we use the Gregorian calendar, which is a refinement of the Julian calendar.

Before Julius Caesar's reform, no correcting adjustments were made to the calendar. When we consider the four thousand years between Caesar's time and the time of creation, almost thirty-two days have to be dropped to make the seasons start when they should. By making these adjustments, Ussher arrived at the date of October 23, not September 21. However, when the Gregorian calendar corrections are applied to the Julian date of October 23, 4004 BC, we get the Gregorian date September 21, 4004 BC, which is the normal day for the autumnal equinox.

Was Ussher correct?

Is there any way that we can verify Ussher's date for creation? There is a passage in Amos that is quite interesting. Around 800 BC Amos made the following prediction in Amos 8:9–10 (NKJV): And it shall come to pass in that day, says the Lord God, that I will make the sun go down at noon, and I will darken the earth in broad daylight; I will turn your feasts into mourning, and all your songs into lamentation; I will bring sackcloth on every waist, and baldness on every head; I will make it like mourning for an only son, and its end like a bitter day.

Many contend that the ancient Jews used a lunar calendar before the Babylonian captivity. If this is so, then Jewish feasts such as the Feast of Pentecost, the Feast of Unleavened Bread and the Feast of Tabernacles would occur about the middle of the month around a full moon. You can never get a solar eclipse when the moon is full! A lunar calendar would make the seasons drift by up to 30 days. Since the Levitical system was based on the agricultural cycle, you could very easily end up, in some years, celebrating the Feast of First Fruits after the entire crop had been harvested. At the other extreme, you might hold the feast before any crop was ready to harvest, which really makes a mockery of the feast. In order for this feast system to work reliably, you must follow the solar year so that the seasons start when they are supposed to and harvests occur about the same time each year.

Ussher states on page 9 in the preface of his *Annals of the World*, "Moreover, we find that the years of our forefathers, the years of the ancient Egyptians and Hebrews, were the same length as the Julian year. It consisted of twelve months containing thirty days each. (It cannot be proven that the Hebrews used lunar months before the Babylonian captivity.) Five days were added after the twelfth month each year. Every four years, six days were added after the twelfth month."[2]

The testimony of so many ancient writers seems to confirm the antiquity (extreme age) of the use of the Julian year—that is, three hundred and sixty-five days with the addition of one extra day every four years. Hence, Ussher had very good reasons for selecting the length of the year that he did. In fact, modern scholarship recognizes this. In 1940 W. G. Waddell translated the works of Manetho, an Egyptian priest of the third century BC, and has the following translation for a portion of the work: "Saites added 12 hours to the month, to make its length 30 days; he added 6 days to the year, which thus comprised of 365 days."[3]

On this passage Waddell has the following footnote: "The addition of 5 days (not 6 as above) to the short year of 360 days was made long before the Hyksos age: it goes back to at least the Pyramid Age and probably earlier. The introduction of the calendar, making an artificial reconciliation of lunar and solar years, perhaps as early as 4236 BC, is believed to give the earliest fixed date of human history."[4]

What the writer is saying is that the calendar, which we now attribute to Julius Caesar, is of very early origin, and it likely dates back to the beginning of civilization. Ussher agrees and, by using the Bible, arrives at the date of 4004 BC for the beginning of civilization, not 4236 BC. (The point being made is that both agreed on the length of the year and that the Julian year is of great antiquity.)

Conclusion

We have seen that Ussher had logical and historically valid reasons for arriving at the year, and even his proposed beginning date of creation. These were not wild guesses of some illiterate

Ussher figured that the earth was created on October 3rd, 4004 B.C. Since he was a big wheel in the church, hardly anyone questioned his "date," at least not for a long while.

One... Two... Three...

bishop counting on his fingers and toes, as progressive creationist Dr. Hugh Ross disrespectfully alleged in one of his organization's cartoon. When we defer to the Bible as our authoritative basis for the areas on which it touches, it will prove itself without fail.

As the Scripture states: let God be true but every man a liar (Romans 3:4).

A summary of how Ussher arrived at the year of creation

The following timeline shows a simplified version of how Ussher used chronologies in Genesis 5 and 11, together with other Bible passages, to arrive at the year of creation.

Date	Event	Scripture	Age of earth
4004 BC	Creation	Gen. 1:1–31	0
3874 BC	Seth born when Adam was 130	Gen. 5:3	130 yrs.
3769 BC	Enos born when Seth was 105	Gen. 5:6	235 yrs.
3679 BC	Cainan born when Enos was 90	Gen. 5:9	325 yrs.
3609 BC	Mahalaleel born when Cainan was 70	Gen. 5:12	395 yrs.
3544 BC	Jared born when Mahalaleel was 65	Gen. 5:15	460 yrs.
3382 BC	Enoch born when Jared was 162	Gen. 5:18	622 yrs.
3317 BC	Methuselah born when Enoch was 65	Gen. 5:21	687 yrs.
3130 BC	Lamech born when Methuselah was 187	Gen. 5:25	874 yrs.
2948 BC	Noah born when Lamech was 182	Gen. 5:28	1,056 yrs.
2446 BC	Shem born when Noah was 502	Gen. 11:10	1,558 yrs.
2348 BC	Flood when Noah was 600	Gen. 7:6	1,656 yrs.
2346 BC	Arphaxad born when Shem was 100	Gen. 11:10	1,658 yrs.
2311 BC	Salah born when Arphad was 35	Gen. 11:12	1,693 yrs.
2281 BC	Eber born when Salah was 30	Gen. 11:14	1,723 yrs.
2246 BC	Peleg born when Eber was 34	Gen. 11:16	1,758 yrs.
2217 BC	Reu born when Peleg was 30	Gen. 11:18	1,787 yrs.
2185 BC	Serug born when Reu was 32	Gen. 11:20	1,819 yrs.
2155 BC	Nahor born when Serug was 30	Gen. 11:22	1,849 yrs.
2126 BC	Terah born when Nahor was 29	Gen. 11:24	1,878 yrs.
1996 BC	Abraham born when Terah was 130	Gen. 11:32; 12:4	2,008 yrs.
1921 BC	Abraham enters Canaan at 75	Gen. 12:4	2,083 yrs.

In addition to the chronologies given in Genesis 5 and 11, Ussher used other large periods of time given in several places in the Bible. Below are these large periods of time that Ussher used in his calculations—without going into all the intermediate details as he did.

Date	Event	Scripture	Age of earth
1921 BC	Abraham left Haran	(Gen. 12:10; Exod. 12:40; Gal. 3:17) 430 years to the very day	2,083 yrs.
1491 BC	The Jewish Exodus	(1 Kings 6:1) 479 years— (In the 480th year or after 479 years)	2,513 yrs.
1012 BC	Start of the Temple	(1 Kings 11:42) 38 years— (Solomon reigned 40 years; Temple was started in his 4th year)	2,992 yrs.
974 BC	Jeroboam's golden calves	(Ezekiel 4:4–6) 390 whole years	3,030 yrs.
584 BC	The final deportation of the Jews[2]		3,420 yrs.

1. *The Annals of the World* (modern-day translation) can be purchased from almost any Christian bookstore in the United States, or online at www.AnswersBookstore.com/go/annals-of-world.

2. *The Annals of the World*, pp. 9, 75-76; see Diod.Sic.,l.1.c.50.s.2.1:177; Strabo,l.17.c.1.s.46.8:125; Strabo,l.17.c.1.s.29,8:85; Herodotus.l.2.c.4.1:279; Genesis 7:11,24; 8:3-5,13,14.

3. Waddell, W.G, Manetho, 1:99, Loeb Classical Library, 1940.

4. Ibid; see Childe, V. Gordon, *New Light on the Most Ancient East*, 1934, pp. 5f.

Larry Pierce is a retired computer programmer who greatly enjoys ancient history. This passion led him to spend five years translating *The Annals of the World* from Latin to English. He is also the creator of a sophisticated and powerful Bible program, The Online Bible.

The "god" of an Old Earth

by Ken Ham

The late Carl Sagan, in his book *Contact*, wrote:

> If God is omnipotent and omniscient, why didn't he start the universe out in the first place so it would come out the way he wants? Why is he constantly repairing and complaining? No, there's one thing the Bible makes clear: The biblical God is a sloppy manufacturer. He's not good at design, he's not good at execution. He'd be out of business if there was any competition.[1]

It's easy to understand why Carl Sagan viewed the God of the Bible this way. Sagan believed that the fossil record, with all its death, mutations, disease, suffering, bloodshed and violence, represented millions of years of earth's history. He also saw a world full of death, mutations, disease, suffering, bloodshed, and violence today. So he concluded that any "god" responsible for this seeming mess of life and death could not be all-powerful and all-knowing.

Sagan's view of God is consistent with his belief in an old earth. Once one accepts billions of years for the age of the earth, whether because of belief in slow and gradual processes to form rocks and fossils—and/or a trust in radiometric dating methods as giving accurate ages of rocks[2]—it follows that the fossil record was laid down during hundreds of millions of years, before there were any people (and thus before human sin).

However, the fossil record is not a pretty one! It shows evidence of animals eating each other,[3] of diseases like cancer in their bones,[4] of violence,[4] of plants with thorns[5] and so on.

Sagan's writings show he was familiar with Genesis. What must he have thought when he read that at the end of the sixth day of creation, God pronounced that everything He had made was very good (Genesis 1:31)? How could a very good earth contain diseases like cancer? Didn't the Bible state that thorns came after the curse because of Adam's sin (Genesis 3:18)?

Sagan is not the only one to recognize the true nature of the god of an old earth. Irven DeVore, a Harvard anthropologist, said:

> I personally cannot discern a shred of evidence for a benign cosmic presence . . . I see indifference and capriciousness. What kind of God works with a 99.9 percent extinction rate?[6]

DeVore recognizes that the fossil record is one of massive extinction. If this has stretched over millions of years, enormous numbers of creatures have become extinct—without such a reason as a Flood judgment on man's wickedness. What kind of god would create such a scenario? The god of an old earth can't be a loving God.

The issue was a major one for Charles Darwin, too.[7] How could a God of love allow such horrible processes as disease, suffering, and death for millions of years?

Christians who believe in an old earth (billions of years) need to come to grips with the real nature of the god of an old earth—it is not the loving God of the Bible. Even many conservative, evangelical Christian leaders accept and actively promote a belief in millions and billions of years for the age of rocks. Many have been influenced by the Progressive Creationist movement[8] as represented by its main spokesperson, Hugh Ross. In his book *Creation and Time*, Ross states:

> Could it be that God's purposes are somehow fulfilled through our experiencing the 'random, wasteful, inefficiencies' of the natural realm He created?[9]

Interestingly, the liberal camp points out the inconsistencies in holding to an old earth, yet trying to cling to evangelical Christianity.

For instance, Bishop John Shelby Spong, the former senior Episcopal Bishop in America, states:

> The Bible began with the assumption that God had created a finished and perfect world from which human beings had fallen away in an act of cosmic rebellion. Original sin was the reality in which all life was presumed to live. Darwin postulated instead an unfinished and thus imperfect creation . . . Human beings did not fall from perfection into sin as the Church had taught for centuries . . . Thus the basic myth of Christianity that interpreted Jesus as a divine emissary who came to rescue the victims of the fall from the results of their original sin became inoperative.[10]

Elsewhere:

> The biblical story of the perfect and finished creation from which human beings fell into sin is pre-Darwinian mythology and post-Darwinian nonsense.[10]

Evolutionist Spong obviously believes in millions of years for earth's history. Like the Progressive Creationists, he rejects a global Flood. Because they interpret the rocks in this way, neither Spong nor the Progressive Creationists can hold to a perfect world before sin. Spong makes it clear that the god of an old earth cannot rescue people from a so-called Fall, when no such Fall as Genesis describes really occurred.[11]

The recipient of the Templeton Prize for Progress in Religion, Ian Barbour, professor emeritus at Carleton College, also said recently:

You simply can't any longer say as traditional Christians that death was God's punishment for sin. Death was around long before human beings.[12]

This is an obvious reference to the millions of years associated with the fossil record. The god of an old earth is one that uses death as part of creating—death therefore can't be the penalty for sin—or "the last enemy" (1 Corinthians 15:26).

In 1994, Tom Ambrose, an Anglican Priest, in an article in *The Church of England Newspaper*, succinctly portrayed the real god of an old earth when he stated:

Fossils are the remains of creatures that lived and died for over a billion years before *Homo sapiens* evolved. Death is as old as life itself by all but a split second. Can it therefore be God's punishment for Sin? The fossil record demonstrates that some form of evil has existed throughout time. On the large scale it is evident in natural disasters. The destruction of creatures by flood, ice age, desert and earthquakes has happened countless times. On the individual scale there is ample evidence of painful, crippling disease and the activity of parasites. We see that living things have suffered in dying, with arthritis, a tumor, or simply being eaten by other creatures. From the dawn of time, the possibility of life and death, good and evil, have always existed. At no point is there any discontinuity; there was never a time when death appeared, or a moment when the evil changed the nature of the universe. God made the world as it is . . . evolution as the instrument of change and diversity. People try to tell us that Adam had a perfect relationship with God until he sinned, and all we need to do is repent and accept Jesus in order to restore that original relationship. But perfection like this never existed. There never was such a world. Trying to return to it, either in reality or spiritually, is a delusion. Unfortunately it is still central to much evangelical preaching.[13]

Spong makes it plain (and it's implied by Ambrose) that the Bible clearly teaches that there was a perfect creation, but it is now marred by sin. But they accept the millions-of-years history for the fossil record, so to be consistent, they have to throw out original sin, and death being the penalty for man's rebellion. The god of an old earth cannot therefore be the God of the Bible who is able to save us from sin and death.

Thus Christians who compromise with the millions of years attributed by many scientists to the fossil record, are in that sense seemingly worshipping a different god—the cruel god of an old earth.

The problem with people like Sagan and Darwin was that they didn't understand (or wouldn't accept) that there was a perfect world to begin with—it was very good. God had created the universe to function perfectly within the rules that He had established for it. These rules weren't just for the physical creation, but also for the creatures who were given instructions to follow (Genesis 1:26–31).

God had instructed Adam to tend the Garden of Eden, eating freely of all of the fruit and produce of the garden. There was only one prohibition—he was not to eat of the Tree of the Knowledge of Good and Evil. But Adam rebelled against God, and, in Adam, we rebelled (Romans 5). The resulting judgment of death and the Curse changed the very good world into one that is groaning in pain till now (Romans 8:22). Death, disease, murder, violence, lying, theft, and all other forms of evil entered into the world and into the hearts of all men.

When looking at this present world, Sagan, Darwin, and the others weren't looking at the nature created perfectly by God, but the results of our sin! What a difference. The condition of this world is the fault of all mankind because all mankind has sinned. This includes you. If you stop and think about it, you have lied, stolen, held hatred in your heart, and other violations of God's standard of perfect holiness.

The God of the Bible, the God of mercy, grace and love, sent His one and only Son to be a man (but God nonetheless), to become our sin-bearer so that we could be saved from sin and its final effect of eternal separation from God:

> "For He has made Him who knew no sin, to be sin for us, that we might become the righteousness of God in Him" (2 Corinthians 5:21).

Jesus Christ came to this earth to live a sinless life and to give His life upon the Cross, absorbing God's wrath against sin so that you can be forgiven of your sin if you will repent and put your trust in what He has done, receiving eternal life. He was resurrected to demonstrate His power over death and a reversal of the effects of sin on the earth. That is the message of the gospel. He is coming again to make a new heavens and earth where those who have been given the gift of eternal life will live with Him forever—in a place where there will be no more death or sin forever!

There's no doubt—the god of an old earth destroys the gospel because death is not the result of sin.

Let this be a challenge to the Church to return to the loving, holy, righteous God of the Bible.

Let this also be a challenge for individuals to trust in Christ, receiving the forgiveness of sins and being credited with the righteousness that can only come through Him.

1. Sagan, C., *Contact*, Pocket Books (Simon & Schuster, Inc.), New York, 1985

2. All dating methods are based on assumptions and numerous results conflict with the evolutionary timescale. E.g. see: Austin, S., *Grand Canyon: Monument to Catastrophe*, Institute for Creation Research, Santee, California, 1994. Morris, J.D., *The Young Earth*, Master Books, Green Forest, Arkansas, 1994. Snelling, A.A., "Radioactive 'Dating' in Conflict!" *Creation* 20(1):24–27, 1997

3. E.g. ground up dinosaur bones were found in the fossil dung of another dinosaur: *Nature* 393(6686):680–682, 1998

4. Tanke, D.H. & Rothschild, B.M., *Paleopathology*, Currie P.J. & Padian K., Ed., *Encyclopedia of Dinosaurs*, Academic Press, San Diego, California, pp. 525–530, 1997

5. Banks, H.P., *Evolution and Plants of the Past*, Wadsworth Publishing Company, Inc., Belmont, California, pp. 9–10, 1970

6. DeVore, I., "Astronomy might be refashioning images of God," *Times-News Weekender*, May 1, 1999. This commonly cited figure is exaggerated—it is based on the evolutionary assumption concerning the many transitional forms that "must have existed'(!). There are only about 250,000 known fossil species

7. Desmond, A. & Moore, J., *Darwin*, Warner Books, New York, p. 479, 1991. See also Brentnall, J.M. and Grigg, R.M., "Darwin's slippery slide into unbelief," *Creation* 18(1):34–37, 1995

8. Typical of this movement would be their adherence to the following beliefs: Big Bang; billions of years for the age of the earth and universe; days of creation are long periods of time; Noah's Flood a local event; race of soulless "humanoids" before Adam and Eve; death and disease existed before sin

9. Ross H., *Creation and Time*, Nav Press Publishing Group, Colorado Springs, Colorado, p. 88, 1994

10. Bishop John Shelby Spong, Episcopal Bishop of Newark, "A Call for a New Reformation," from home page for the Episcopal Diocese of Newark, September 4, 1999. For a thorough refutation of Spong's many errors and outright heresies, see Bott M.R., and Sarfati J.D., "What's wrong with Bishop Spong?," *Apologia* 4(1):3–27, 1995

11. Consistently, Spong also denies virtually every other Christian doctrine—including the bodily Resurrection and the Virginal Conception of Christ etc., and says that homosexual acts are acceptable

12. Cited in Lieblich, J., "Searching for answers: Templeton Prize winner bridges science and faith," *Dayton Daily News*, Religion Section, Saturday March 13, 1999

13. Ambrose, T., "Just a pile of old bones," *The Church of England Newspaper*, A Current Affair Section, Friday October 21, 1994